A SUSSEX HIGHLANDER

THE MEMOIRS OF SERGEANT WILLIAM KENWARD 1767 - 1828

EDITED BY
DENIS KENWARD AND
RICHARD NESBITT-DUFORT

whydown books

Published in 2005 by Whydown Books Ltd
Sedlescombe, East Sussex TN33 0RN

© Denis Kenward 2005

All rights reserved. No part of this book may be reprinted or reproduced or utilised in any form or by any electronic, mechanical, or other means now known or hereafter invented, including photocopying and recording, or in any information storage or retrieval system, without permission in writing from the publishers.

ISBN 1-874262-07-1

www.whydownbooks.com

Printed by
Windmill Press
Hadlow Down, Uckfield
East Sussex TN22 4ET

For Rowena

Contents

List of Illustrations
List of Maps
Acknowledgements
Foreword
Introduction

William Kenward's Preface
Chapter 1   1767 - 1789   Early Days and India
Chapter 2   1790 - 1793   Into Action
Chapter 3   1794 - 1799   The End of Tipu
Chapter 4   1800 - 1802   The Pacification of the South
Chapter 5   1803   A Change of Scene
Chapter 6   1804 - 1806   A New Enemy
Chapter 7   1807 - 1809   A Different War
Chapter 8   1810 - 1815   An Old Soldier
Letters Home

William Kenward's Campaigns
Bibliography
Index

Illustrations

1. The Uniform of the 75th Highland Regiment on formation in 1787.
2. An East Indiaman off the Cape of Good Hope, 1790.
3. A contemporary print of the Assault on Seringapatam in 1799.
4. General Robert Craufurd.
5. A Sergeant of the 75th Highlanders about 1799 in Southern India
6. The Death of Tipu.
7. General Sir David Baird.
8. A contemporary Satire on the Walcheren Expedition.
9. Moons Farm, Piltdown.
10. Fletching Church and graveyard, with the Inscription on William Kenward's gravestone.
11. A page of the Memoirs.
12. The Kenward Family Tree.

Maps

1. Southern India in the 1790's.
2. Seringapatam in 1799.
3. Northern India in 1805.
4. North West Spain in 1808-09.
5. Walcheren in 1809.
6. The Area around Fletching, East Sussex.

Acknowledgements

The editors would like to thank the following individuals and institutions for their interest and help in preparing these memoirs for publication: Douglas Anderson, Nina Dufort, Brig. John Hemsley, Adrian Hill, Anne Kennaway, the Kenward family, David Penn, Jenny Shaw, Chris Whittick, the Royal United Services Institute, the National Army Museum, the Gordon Highlanders Museum, the Duke of Wellington's Regimental Museum and the East Sussex County Record Office.

Picture Acknowledgements

1. Douglas N. Anderson.
2. Courtesy of the Director, National Maritime Museum, Greenwich.
3 & 4. Courtesy of the Director, National Army Museum, London.
5. Douglas N. Anderson.
6. Reproduced from Nolan's History of the British Empire (Copyright unknown).
7 & 8. Courtesy of the Director, National Army Museum.
9. Kenward family.
10. James Hayllar.
11 & 12. Kenward family.
Cover. Douglas N. Anderson.

Foreword

When Mr. Wood, the village schoolmaster of Newick in Sussex, was teaching his pupils the three Rs, I wonder if he ever imagined that a quarter of a millenium later the memoirs of one of the small boys in front of him would surface and be read with excitement by not only the people of Newick and nearby Fletching, but by military historians throughout the land. William Kenward's clear copperplate handwriting, his command of English, and his descriptive powers are a tribute to Mr. Wood and he had a knowledge of Shakespeare and of English history at a time (mid-eighteenth century) when literacy among country boys must have been a rarity.

Posterity should be grateful to Mr. Wood, and of course William Kenward, for providing us with one of the rare accounts of a soldier's career, the more authentic since it is written, entirely without self-glorification, from the lower ranks. He gives us tantalizing glimpses of the severe life of a soldier in India and the hardships he endured, from lice, fearsome ants, and widespread sickness, to his struggles to extract his due prize money, even pay, from unscrupulous army agents. Yet he is most loyal, to his regiment and to his officers, paying tribute to their bravery when due, but equally critical of their shortcomings.

The army that he joined was very different to the army that defeated Napoleon - a contemporary account recalls that " each colonel of a regiment managed it according to his own notions, or neglect altogether ...... no uniformity of drill or movement'.

However, while William played his part at the battle of Seringapatam, a certain Colonel Arthur Wellesley in command of the reserve was forming his own plans for the future army.

Not only does William provide corroboration for existing

accounts, but he adds his own colourful touches. I must leave the reader to discover them, but I cannot resist one example : as the towering General Baird led his troops through the breach at Seringapatam, his biographer has him bellowing, "Now my brave fellows, follow ME and prove yourselves worthy of the name of British soldiers!" William has him shouting " Tippoo - or no Baird! Follow me, my lads , and we'll soon shave him!"

As I stood with Denis Kenward by William's grave in the churchyard at Fletching, eerily by torchlight, I was moved by thoughts of this man who gave his life over to service for his country, gaining his strength from his comrades and his regiment, and from his roots in Fletching where his family had farmed the same land for many generations. I felt great sadness that his regiment had been fragmented beyond recognition, and that our great traditions of farming have been reduced to form-filling and grant applications. But the fields and woods of Fletching will always be there, and there will always be William Kenwards to serve their country.

Alasdair Campbell
Late Major, 5th Royal Inniskilling Dragoon Guards
Fletching 2005

Introduction

The Kenward family has lived, farmed and worked in the vicinity of the old village of Fletching in Sussex for centuries, and many are still there. The ancient farm named Moons at Piltdown in the parish of Fletching was in the family for generations, and they were also "customary tenants" of the adjacent Manor of Barkham.

At the end of the Second World War a Mr. F. de Verteuil (aka Freddie Bannister) lodged in Fletching, and was clearing out an old desk belonging to his landlady, Mabel Kenward, when he found a cache of old documents, including a handwritten notebook and numerous letters in the same hand. Unfortunately, mice had made inroads into the letters, but enough remained to show that they had been written by an ancestor of the family in the period 1790 to 1815. The book was undamaged and Mr. de Verteuil made a typed copy. At the time little notice was taken of this archive, but several decades later Denis Kenward, who was a direct descendant of William Kenward's brother John, typed out the surviving parts of the letters, intending at some time to properly investigate the story. This was of one William Kenward, who served in the Army in India and in Europe during the Napoleonic Wars, and retired to become a Chelsea Pensioner in 1815. Realising that his reminiscences were unusual, and that no other family members had served His Majesty, William had set down his memories for his family and their descendants.

In 1990 the local historical society published in their magazine extracts of the story together with details of the family history, and noted that William Kenward was buried in Fletching churchyard, but little attention was paid to what is in fact a remarkable story. Some years later Denis Kenward was contacted by an acquaintance who was intrigued by the story, and was in a position to turn it into a book.

It is a fact that memoirs of those who served in the ranks of the army of the period are rare, and nearly all these concern the Peninsular War and Waterloo. For a memoir of a soldier who lived and fought through the Mysore and Mahratta Wars, including the taking of Seringapatam, returned to England and then survived the retreat to Corunna and the malaria-devastated Walcheren expedition to be still unknown to the public is remarkable.

An orphan, a volunteer who enlisted at the age of 20 after running away from an apprenticeship, he came to be the sole survivor of his draft of 110 men sent to India in 1789. He worked his way up to become the Pay and Orderly Room Sergeant of the 75th Highland Regiment of Foot, then exchanged into the 76th Foot in the same capacity before returning to England in 1806. After two more campaigns he became unfit for active service in 1811 and was transferred to a Veterans Battalion for garrison duty. He became a Chelsea out-pensioner in early 1815, and returned to live in Lewes in Sussex near his family. His discharge document survives, detailing his service, and recording that he was only wounded once, by an arrow in the knee in India. His health however had been seriously affected by his long years of strenuous service in dangerous and disease-ridden climates, and he died in 1828 at the age of 61.

His memoirs, backed up by some of his contemporary letters home, show that he was literate, well-informed and highly observant. They shed a fascinating light on how the British conquered India, and he is not shy of commenting on the strange customs and characteristics of the natives and the shortcomings of officers and the Army system. He was of course in a very good position to understand the workings of the military of the time, and not slow to work the system himself when he could. His lengthy descriptions of India, its peoples, flora and fauna were probably aimed at educating his younger relations, bearing in mind that in the early years of the nineteenth century the great majority of Sussex people had not travelled more than a score of miles from where they were born.

The letters were nearly all sent to William Kenward's elder brother John (JK), who was the head of the family and lived at Moons Farm, Fletching. However, one was written to Mr Isard, his old apprentice master at East Grinstead. His correspondence with John was obviously not all one way, as he did receive some news from home, although complaining frequently that his brother was a poor correspondent. He obviously believed that the rest of the family still thought of him as a n'er-do-well and a black sheep, something which evidently troubled him greatly for a long time, and there is an increasingly fatalistic tone to the letters. However he remained very attached to his family, and sought their news avidly. It would seem from the letters that his first visit home was not until Christmas 1806, nearly twenty years after he left under a cloud.

WK does not often say much about his personal activities, preferring to describe actions dispassionately, but it is obvious from the text that he was frequently in the thick of the action, and personally took part in many of the sieges and assaults he describes. His survival is therefore all the more remarkable. Apart from a few lapses over dates and place names, his recollections are quite accurate, and nearly all military details can be corroborated from other sources. His words remain a moving testament to a time of bravery, hardship, squalor, disease and corruption, through which the fortitude and endurance of the British soldier stands out.

Editorial Note.

The editors have only made minor changes to the original text in the interests of readability, kept the original spelling as far as practicable, corrected dates and place names in a few instances, and added explanatory and historical notes where appropriate. William Kenward is referred to throughout the notes as WK, an abbreviation he often used himself. The text has also been divided into chapters which do not appear in the original. His rather fragmentary surviving letters have been included as an appendix, as they add considerable detail and sometimes some flesh to his often rather impersonal memoirs. It is unfortunate that no letters from his brother survive, but perhaps this is to be expected, given the vicissitudes of campaigning.

William Kenward's Preface

FAITH, HOPE CHARITY.

To my Dear & near Relations

Kinsmen,

As I am the only man of the Family or name that I know of, who ever had the Honour of serving His Majesty, (or to use the words of some and opinions of many) that ever was Fool enough to disgrace himself and Family, by becoming a Robber, Murderer and a Runaway, to serve his King and Country (for the sake of a bounty of thirty Shillings) - I shall present you with a short sketch of the first 47 or 48 Years of my life, be it more or less, And if you feel disposed to peruse it, slip on your Spectacles, take a good Quid of Tobacco and fall to it. And should you find any amusement in it, as also to pass away an Idle hour, you will receive the same reward in reading, I had for writing it.

And Finally should you have FAITH enough to credit its contents I HOPE you will have the CHARITY to excuse the Presumption and Ill Performance of an Illiterate Penman. I Remain
> Dear Couzins
> With Regard and Esteem
> Yours Sincerely
> W.Kenward
> late Sergt. in H.M. 75th and 76th Regiment
> and 2nd. R V Battalion.

Chapter 1

Early Days and Arrival in India
1767 - 1789

Born in the Parish of Newick in the County of Sussex, in the year 1769 my mother died some short time before my Father, which latter event took place when I was about Four Years of Age in consequence of which, myself, Three Brothers and three Sisters became Orphans. This afflicting loss of our Parents was however by Gods Providence little felt by any of us, not by myself at those tender Years scarcely knowing what might have been the feelings of my elder Brothers and Sisters on this distressing occasion I leave to those who have felt similar adversity. My Father fell a victim to the small Pox in the year I believe of 1772 or 3, and it was my good fortune (together with an elder Brother & Sister) to be taken to our Grandfathers, then a Farmer at Barkham in Fletching, but which he soon after removed from, to his own land at Moons in the same Parish, and shortly after, by the death of our Venerable and beloved Grandfather we a second time lost a Parent. My Uncle William succeeded him by Will and under him I was treated with all the marks of a tender Guardian, and which continued during his life and did not end with his Death, having left me a considerable Legacy. But how worthy I proved myself of his many bounties will appear in this Narrative.

After having received a suitable Education for a Tradesman from Mr. Wood schoolmaster of Newick whom I attended some years by my Uncles generosity, I was Apprenticed in 1784 to Mr.

Isard Breeches maker and Glover at E.Grinstead for (I believe) 5 years, but which previous to its termination I ran from through an Unlawful and Predal act, which although not of a henious nature, yet in due time was convinced of its Impropriety, by the just afflictions of the hand of God which afterwards accompanied me, and altho not punished according to my deserts felt in some degree the just anger of the Almighty upon me, and which undoubtedly sooner or later will overtake all those who wander from God, Forsake their Parents wholesome admonition and become Dupes to that Wicked Trinity, the World, the Flesh and the Devil.

After having for a few months followed my trade in different parts of the Kingdom, wen I could obtain any work, which at that time I found very dull, and no doubt was often refused work wen others would have obtained it, as my appearance (although decently dressed) prejudiced me in their Opinion. I was often asked whether I was not a runaway Prentice, which you may be sure I always denied and even had the hardened Guilt afterwards to deny on Oath at Chatham, where to add to my sorrows I enlisted for a Soldier in the 75th Highld. Regiment raised for India service and then on its Passage. I joined them in Bombay the Augt. following.

The 75th Highland Regiment, or Abercromby's Highlanders, had been one of four new regiments, two English and two Scottish, raised in 1787 specifically for service in India. Embodied at Stirling, they had sailed for India the next year and WK's draft was probably their first batch of reinforcements. Recruiting at this time was fraught with difficulty, as the army was held in low regard by all in England. Fortescue notes about these regiments 'that the difficulty in raising them was so great that leave was given to accept prisoners from Gloucester gaol, dismissed seamen, and even out-pensioners of Chelsea Hospital as recruits.' The situation in the Highlands was better however, as there the army was considered a reasonable calling for a respectable man. The then bounty of three guineas and the miserly pay subject to excessive stoppages, was quite insufficient to attract good recruits elsewhere. Ireland was regarded as a last resort, as although numerous recruits could be found there, the numbers of deserters was equally great. It is most unlikely that the army would have taken any notice of the possibility that WK had broken an apprenticeship, given the opportunity to enlist such a fine recruit. Furthermore, it was not uncommon for runaway apprentices to enlist. A young bricklayer's apprentice from Dorset called William Lawrence, who became a sergeant in the 40th Regiment and dictated his story many years later, was barely fifteen when he took the King's Shilling in 1805.

In January 1790, it is recorded that the regiment's ranks were made up as follows -

Scottish   437
English   73
Irish   33
Foreigners 5

the officers being in about the same proportion.

The other Regiments formed for Indian service, and paid for, albeit very reluctantly, by the East India Company, were the 74th, 76th and 77th. Of the Regiments in which WK served, the 75th eventually became part of the Gordon Highlanders and the 76th part of the Duke of Wellington's Regiment. The 74th became part of the Highland Light Infantry and the 77th the Middlesex Regiment.

110 Recruits embarked on the Ponsborne Indiaman in the month of February 1789 among which number was myself, and after a tedious passage of better than six months arrived at our destination, having in the course of the voyage only called at St. Iago, one of the Canary Islands for a trifling refit, for which we suffered in a Gale a few days before we made that Island.

Here we remained about a fortnight and proceeded on our Voyage without any particular Occurrence until arrival off the Cape of Good Hope. It was there God awaited us in order to call such as lived in their sins to a sincere repentance and to convince us that the good success of a Voyage depends solely on Heaven. We were however happily delivered from our fears after about a Fort-night buffeting with furious winds and seas, without any material Injury by the calm and moderate weather which succeeded, and which accompanied us the remainder of the Voyage.

We buried (or rather cast overboard,) during the Passage only one soldier and a sailor, owing no doubt to the humane care and attention of the Captain of the ship whose name was Thomas. He was certainly a most excellent character, which was a great mercy to us, having no Officer on board to whom had it been necessary we might have appealed to check the Tyrany of a Vicious Commander.

> *WK was right to be thankful for a relatively safe and uneventful voyage in an well-found East Indiaman, even though soldiers had to travel in the steerage, all other accommodation being reserved for paying civilian passengers. Conditions on troop transports were usually appalling, and to quote Fortescue - " In truth it is difficult in these days to realise the perils and discomforts patiently endured by officers and men in leaky transports, when frequently they could not sleep dry for weeks together. Not the least of the dangers was the drunkenness and incompetence of the masters and mates, which on at least one occasion compelled a captain of infantry to take command and navigate a ship from the West Indies to England." Fortescue was writing a hundred years ago.*

On our arrival at HeadQuarters we were treated with much lenity by Captain (late General) Crawfurd, then in the immediate

Command of the Regiment, (The Field Officers all holding Staff Situations.) For many weeks we were not even permitted to expose ourselves to a Vertical Sun as the severe effects thereof on the constitutions of new arrivals, had been experienced by those who preceeded us, many of whom had gone to whence there is no return, and many of us, altho carefully guarded from running to excess, by eating the Country fruits or drinking its Intoxicating and Pernicious liquor, were soon taken ill, some with Fever, others with Bowel and different Complaints, so that a very great majority of our number brought with us were in their graves before a residence of a few Years in India.

The Regiment's Colonel, Col. Robert Abercromby, had been appointed Governor of Bombay, and took command of the Bombay Army for the operations in Mysore. At this time the British forces in India were still divided into three Armies, based on the three East India Company Presidencies, Bombay, Madras and Calcutta in Bengal, the first two being subordinate to Calcutta. Coordination between the armies was however often poor because of distance, terrain and personality conflicts. The 75th were part of the Bombay Army.

Captain Robert Craufurd, known later as "Black Bob", became the famous commander of the Light Division in the Peninsular War and was killed at the storming of Ciudad Rodrigo in 1812. He had been attached to the Prussian Army earlier in his career, admired their methods and was in consequence a fierce disciplinarian. His methods did not go down well with the Regiment initially, and it was noted that 'Scotsmen would not easily be brought to bear German punishments'. However, Craufurd was respected for his impartiality and for leading from the front, and the Regimental History says, with understandable pride, that the Regiment became one of the best trained in the army, 'as remarkable for good conduct in quarters as for gallantry in the field and smartness on parade'.

Bombay is a small Island, distant from the main land but a few leagues. The Inhabitants are of different Nations, Languages and Religions. The Mahomedans (or Musselmen) however are here the most numerous, and are chiefly soldiers or sailors altho there are many Artisans and Husbandmen among them. Also on the coast many Fishermen. They are in general more Industrious and less treacherous than their other Neighbours.

The Brahmin and Gentoo caste are also Very numerous. They are a Tribe (or Tribes) of Idolators, whose Priest (which are many) appears to have only the Aim of leading the Vulgar from the Path of God to enrich themselves on their plunder. They being so numerous are a great burthen to the poor by whose liberality they are all maintained, being considered Holy men. They marry only in their own Tribes.

Some of those Bramins withdraw from the converse of Mankind, there being Anchorets among them living in caves and Deserts and yet with all their pretended sanctity are a most wicked set of wretches. They are the greatest Imposters in the World, dayly inventing fabulous Stories which they pass among the Ignorant people for so many Incomprehensible misteries; they persuade them that their Idols eat like men, and in order that they may be more plentifully provided with good Cheer, make them of a Gigantic figure with a particular large paunch. Should the People fail in their Offerings (with which the Bramins maintain themselves and familys) they threaten them with the Anger of God.

They believe there is something divine in a Cow to whom they pay adoration, and happy is the dying man, if when expiring he can by any means lay hold of that animals tail, for the soul thus assisted quits the body purified, and sometimes returns into the body of the Cow. This however is seldom indulged but to Superior Spirits, who despise life and die Generously either by throwing themselves from a precipice, by leaping into a lighted pile, or may be trampled to death by the crowd whilst their Idols are carried in Triumph about the City. They believe the souls of the Wicked will in the next Nativity animate the bodies of Swine, Dogs, or some filthy creature. From this belief of Transmigration, they Religiously abstain from eating the flesh of any living Creature, fearing thereby they might feed on a body, informed with a soul, which before, had animated a Parent or some near Relation.

They burn their dead and at the death of a Husband, the wife must Voluntary throw herself on the fatal pile with her dead Husband. I was a spectator of one of those horrid transactions at Brodera in the Province of Guzerat in 1804. The shocking Ceremony was as follows on the Banks of the Tappir river.

The funeral pile being prepared and the dead body of the husband laid thereon the unfortunate Victim soon made her appearance attended by a vast retinue of female relations and Friends, together with her Idolatrous Priest. On arrival at the Pile they commenced singing to a doleful tune. The words I knew not, but was informed it was in praise of the Deceaseds Virtues and the heroic Act about to be Performed by his Widow. After which, attended by females only, she went to a place appointed for her bath were she continued nearly half an hour and returned dressed in a thin robe of white Cambric.

The Priest then anointed her Garment and Hair, which was beautiful and long, with a certain composition made for the purpose chiefly consisting of Sulphur. She then repeats her song with the assistance of her attendance, marches thrice round the Pile and ascends, where with much seeming composure she laid herself down by her dead Husband. The Mob then commenced a hideous shout, clapping of hands, blowing of horns and tingling of bells when one of the Priest handed her a lighted Torch, to which she herself set the Pile on Fire, and it being a sort of Touchwood, and no doubt she was also with Sulphur, became in an Instant in a blaze, and in a few minutes both bodies were consumed.

She appeared to be a young woman about 22 or 23 Years of Age, and of beautiful features. Her husband (had not the hand of death altered his appearance) could not have been far short of 60.

A monument was commenced to be erected over their Ashes before the Attendants departed which was finished in a few days after. This horrid Custom is prohibited in the Companies Territorys but as this Tragic scene took place in the Country of our Allies, the British Commander could not Interfere, although he used all possible means by entreatys to prevent it.

The practice of Suttee or Sati was finally banned throughout Hindu India by the British in 1829, but took some time to stamp out completely.

PERSEES, *(Parsees)* these are an Industrious and very ingenious race of men, consisting of Merchants, Mechanics and Husbandmen, also many trusty servants to Gentlemen. They are excellent Ship Carpenters and by whom the Country Vessels in India are built they perform the whole of that laborious business in a manner to a European surprising. The Saw Axe or Hammer being all used sitting, and to see their method of proceeding one would Imagine a Thousand Years would be insufficient to build a Frigate or Indiaman, yet in a few months they hand them over to Old Neptune as firm and handsomely built as those launched from our English Docks.

They neither burn nor bury their dead, but carry them on an Iron bier to the Sepulchre where they are laid on a Grating (also of Iron) - here they lay exposed to Vultures and other birds of prey till the flesh is devoured. The bones thus disengaged of flesh tumbles through the Grating & remain in a promiscous heap. They are worshipers of Fire and are strict Observers of the rising sun to which they pay Adoration every morning thro the Year either in the Fields, Gardens or on the Tops of their houses but if near the sea, by the Waterside. Should their house and all that is dear and valuable to them take fire they will not attempt to extinguish it even could it be done with a Pint of Water or troden out, but will satisfy any other person well for doing it for them. They offer up their Prayers in the Morning facing the sun and in the Evening towards the Moon.

They are generally very rich and a poor Persee cannot be Known, for should they fail or become unfortunate in trade they are relieved by the bounties of their brethren; they have also many other excellent properties which it would be a credit to the English nation to take example from.

HALALCORES (Commonly called Parias) are a most miserable set of wretches who formerly perhaps were persons of Respectability of either sex, but failing in some little particular or perhaps for some greater offence, are excluded their society, even their nearest relations dare not assist or relieve them. They are therefore obligated to undergo a punishment more severe than Death, or ransom their former Priveledges at an Intolerable sacrifice or Expence. Should they not be able to perform the One or willing to perform the Other, the Priest will pronounce the exclusion together with Damnation. They, from that Instant have only recourse to the humanity of the British or other European Powers trading in India, who employ them in removing Nuisances Dead Animals Privys etc. which the regular sects dare not perform under penalty of the same disgrace or severe punishments. These unfortunate beings are particularly useful in a British Camp assisting the wounded and sick, and many a British Soldier (probably myself) owes his life to the attention of these Outcasts of Eastern Society. After they become thus degraded they immediately throw off the Mask and as before their exclusion they never eat any thing which ever drew breath, now they descend to the other extreme by not only eating what we do, but will not refuse to partake of any animal (clean or unclean) such as Dogs, Cats, Rats etc. In Camp when the Cattle so frequently die for want of Food or Fatigue they are continually cooking and feasting, but should circumstances render it impossible to perform the former they will not want a refreshment by eating the flesh raw.

Should they attempt to regain their Cast by acts of Penance such severe tasks are imposed on them by their Priests as a man in his sober sences would shudder at, such as burning themself thro the body, crawling hundreds of miles on their hands and knees, hanging themselves up on hooks as Beef on the Shambles, keeping their arms extended over their heads for such a number of years, either of which attempts ever after renders them more Objects of Pity, and prevent them ever after from following their usual vocation, and the latter prevents them from ever bringing down their arms to their proper limits and functions. Would not therefore any man in his sences prefer Death to the Obligation of ever appearing with the arms thus extended, which not only deprives him of their use, but renders them objects of ridicule. I dare say those who are able may compound with the Priest according to their ability as they do not care so much for the souls of their transgressors as they do for their own bodies to gratify a greedy and Insatiate Appetite.

Shoemakers called Chucklers (who are also Tanners and Curriers) are of this Caste, but somewhat more respected. Their handling the skins of dead Animals deprives them of the Society they else might have the Honor of being members of. They however care but little for any religion, and their trade, altho considered contemptable, is among the best in India.

The Butchers are from the Mahometans, who are no ways particular as to Punctilous, they detest the Bramin and Gintoos, they have often attempted to prevent the cruel sacrifices these bigoted and Ignorant people make, and would no doubt before this have exterminated them both but for the interference of the British Government.

Having said thus much concerning a race of brutes (for men they cannot be called) shall proceed in my tale.

The casualty rate from disease for newly arrived troops was horrific. WK says that a 'very great majority' succumbed, and only a few years earlier, one unfortunate regiment had lost nearly 90% in their first year. However, if a man survived this period, he was much less likely to die of disease later. WK notes that he probably owed his life to the ministrations of the Halalcores when he was ill himself.

Chapter 2

Campaigning in Mysore
1790 - 1793

A few months after our arrival we received orders to be held in readiness for Field service and embarked soon after under the command of the brave General Hartly, we were landed at Aicotta to assist an old and faithful Allie the King of Travancore. We however landed at a time when it was impossible to commence our intended Operations as the rainy season was just set in and we were in consequence obliged to construct Temporary Barracks. The heavy and incessant rain which fell for many months, the like of which we were never before exposed to, carried of upwards of a hundred men of the 75th in a few weeks, the remainder little better than dying men, from fevers, Dysentry, etc. oblidged us to remove to Cochin at that time in possession of the Dutch with whom we were at peace, and permitted to remain the rest of the Winter, when from more comfortable Food and Lodging the greater number were sufficiently recovered to take the Field the next Spring. During the interval of our unavoidable Inactivity our Enemy Tippoo made a rapid progress in his conquest. Cranganore a considerable Fortress of Malabar was bombarded and taken, Chitwa and Chowghaut soon after experienced the same fate, and the poor King (or Rajah's) forces panic struck fled from the enemy without ever after making any or a very feeble resistance. The season being sufficiently advanced for our taking the Field, with about 1500 European and Natives and a small park of Artillery, in a few weeks we not only retook all those Garrisons, but completely defeated his Army under the Command of Cumerdieu Cawn, of upwards 25000 at Trevanagary with only a loss of about 14 Killed, and Thirty wounded.

This action, under Col. Hartley, took place on the 10th December 1790, and together with Abercromby's capture of Cannanore, secured Malabar. It was the first major engagement of the 75th, and earned the particular thanks of Governor-General Cornwallis, as well as those of the Government of Bombay. Cummer-ud-din Khan was one of Tipu's senior commanders.

The Madras Army under General Floyd had also by this time performed wonders, the Cavalry cut them down by Hundreds, and the small Galloping Guns (the first ever used in India and which were supplied to each Brigade) threw the Enemy in such confusion that they could not for a while be again brought to face us in the Field. The Madras Infantry also in their turn took from the Enemy the Garrisons of Paulgautchery and Coimbatore which was an afflicting loss to Tippoo, the former being a strong and regular built Garrison, and with the exception of his Capital, was the second in his country. These Garrisons were left ill mand., particularly Coimbatore which was only defended by a Company of Native Infantry, with a very few Artillery Gunners. The Enemy seeing a favourable opportunity besieged them and after a brave resistance of some weeks with a handful of men, a Capitulation was agreed upon and signed by which Lieut. Chambers and his Party were to deliver up the Garrison, and permitted to withdraw his men into the Companys Territorys. This however was not afterwards admitted by Tippoo altho specified in the Articles; they were all marched Prisoners of War to Seringapatam where we shall leave them no doubt miserably treated and bemoaning their unhappy fate till the following Year.

Coimbatore was besieged from 11th June to 11 August 1790, and again from 6th October to 6th November, when it was surrendered, both Chambers and the only other British officer being wounded.

As the Madras Armys duty was to scour the Eastern part of the Sultans Territory, so ours was to protect that part of the South belonging to our Allie, and take such Garrisons from him as was in our power to succeed in, and which having accomplished marched to join General Abercromby who was more Westward, and with the 77th Regt and a few Battalions of Seapoys had the good fortune to become Master of Cannonore with very small loss.

Cannonore was a tollerable strong Garrison near the sea. The town is about a mile distant but without defence. This beautiful Country was governed by a Woman and had previously been for many Ages. For what reason I knew not the present queen (called the Bibbee) of Cannonore is said to have been the Daughter of a British General, but I know not the truth thereof. Be it as it may, she had much the resemblance of an European and to whom she had a great partiality and shewed some favours, I mean to the Officers.

Since the Conquest of Malabar this Important Garrison has been retained by the English allowing a Princly Pension to her Copper coloured Majesty who most probably is better satisfied than managing the Affairs of its Government.

After joining Genl. Abercromby, we both made a formidable appearance. Our next movement was toward Mysore, but numerous Obstacles seemed to present themselves, sufficient to check the Spirit of any man but our brave Commander. After a few days marches, we arrived at the foot of the Poodicherune Ghauts (mountains) to ascend which with our Field Pieces seemed an impossibility, from the great height of the numerous mountains before us being in some parts nearly perpendicular. However, by hard labour we cut a road, and by the assistance of

Elephants succeeded in about two months in getting up our Guns and the other requisites for the Siege of Seringapatam.

On 22nd February 1791, the Bombay Army, consisting of the 73rd, 75th, and 77th Regiments, a regiment of Bombay Europeans, and seven battalions of sepoys, about 9,000 soldiers in all, left the coast for Mysore, but took eleven weeks to haul themselves and their siege guns over the mountains. The artillery and stores needed 12,000 bullocks as well as the elephants. It was a remarkable feat to make a road for the heavy guns through 50 miles of thick jungle, soft paddy fields and steep mountains.

Fortunately, the Rajah of Coorg, a small mountain state adjacent to Malabar, had refused to acknowledge Tipu's suzerainty, and openly assisted the Bombay Army's passage through the Ghauts.

This unavoidable delay was a serious Misfortune to us as the rainy season was rapidly Approaching, the Thunder and Lightning which is the forerunner of it had already commenced and some showers had fallen when we again attempted to proceed to our destined point. We had marched through the Caraka Rajahs boundry to the Sultans borders, and arrived at his deserted fort of Periapatam; here we awaited the Orders of General Meadows who was already before the Capital (and had made some progress after capturing on his Route the strong Garrison of Bangalore) when the violent and long expected rain came down in Torrents, which obliged the General to relinquish his plan of Operations for that year, and from the rapid swelling of the Cavary and other rivers which he must necessarily pass to commence a hasty retreat to Fort St. George, at the same time ordering us to descend the Ghauts and Winter at Cananore. This gave great pleasure to the Tyrant, but we did not long leave him to rejoice at our Ill success.

> Gen. Abercromby's force did not arrive at Periapatam until the 15th May, but unfortunately was not in communication with Lord Cornwallis and Gen. Medows, whose Madras Army was besieging Seringapatam only forty miles away. Cornwallis sent orders for Abercromby to retreat to Malabar on the 21st May, still unaware of the Bombay troops position, and started his own retreat towards Madras a few days later.

As we were conveying a large supply of Biscuits, Rice, Spirits, etc. for the supply of both Armys it was a serious loss to Government as the greater part was damaged or totally spoiled, and considerable quantities left behind. Our great Guns were buried and had the good fortune to find the next Campaign that the sagacious enemy had not found out the places of their concealments. The retreat of both Armys, altho conducted with much skill, was attended with considerable loss, the greatest felt on our part was the loss of several brave Comrades.

> The "great guns" were the siege artillery that they had hauled to the top of the Ghauts with so much effort. When the army returned the next season, the guns were emplaced to guard the pass, and another siege train used in the assault on Seringapatam.
> A contemporary account lists the huge numbers of bullocks needed to transport siege artillery across India. One twenty four pounder siege gun required 155 bullocks, and these bullocks in turn needed 465 more to carry fodder for them all for a month. Large parts of Southern India had to be denuded of draught animals to supply the huge numbers needed.

During our stay at Periapatam our General Hospital was established in the Fort, by which means the sick were more comfortably provided for than was possible in a wet Camp, but on the night of our retreat which commenced with private Orders about 10 o'clock, either the Principle Medical Officer misunderstood the Order, or had not the means of Conveyance for those unable to proceed. We therefore had proceeded many miles on our retreat before the sick were apprized of it.

At break of day next morning the Guard left with them and all who could by any means move attempted to follow. Those who could not fell into the hands of the Enemy, most of whom were murdered, and those who escaped death were carried prisoners to Seringapatam where they experienced a severe but providentially short Captivity.

The Sick and Guard who were following us were continually harassed by the Enemy until they joined us, and a very few of their number but were slain or made Prisoners.

The 75th were acting as rearguard for the Bombay Army during this retreat. The conditions were most unpleasant as the monsoon had broken, and, as in most retreats, morale was low. However, the lack of organisation evidenced by the failure to ensure the wounded were moved was inexcusable.

A Corporal of the Company to which I then belonged (Colonels) was left for dead by the Enemy on the road for two days, and was observed by a party of the Rajahs men and brought to our lines, with scarcely any signs of life, his Scull nearly cleft in two, and a severe wound in his Shoulder, by which he had lost much blood. Any attempt to recover him seemed hopeless and in a day or two he was supposed to have Died. He was accordingly laid out, toes tied and wrapt up in his burial Garb, but on taking him to his Grave which was already dug, some signs of life appeared. The party therefore returned with him to the Hospital, where by great attention he soon recovered and did duty with the Regiment many years after. The severe wound of his head however, in the end proved fatal to him. He had many and repeated intervals of Insanity in one of which he blew out his brains with his own Fuzee (being then Serjeant) whilst on the Main Guard duty in the Garrison of Bombay.

A battalion of British infantry consisted of up to ten companies, each between 80 and 100 strong, although on active service they were often smaller. Of these, two were called 'flank' companies, being the Grenadier company on the right of the line, and the Light company on the left, the others being known as 'battalion' companies. Although WK does not say so, the flank companies tended to contain the fitter and better trained men. These companies were often detached for special tasks, sometimes with the flank companies of other regiments. Commanders therefore had the use of better trained and more flexible bodies of men for more difficult tasks, but this sometimes diluted the quality of the rest of the battalion.

The Colonel still nominally commanded one of the battalion companies, but in practice, a junior captain was in day to day command. Some sergeants carried a fusee or fusil, which was a short musket, instead of the usual pike. About this time the India pattern musket, which was three inches shorter than the old model, was introduced by the East India Company.

The Army of the East India Company, mainly officered by English and Scots, consisted of battalions of European soldiers, many foreign mercenaries as well as British, and Native troops called sepoys. The Company officers were regarded as the social and professional inferiors of the King's officers of the British Army, although they often commanded joint forces.

A 'Regiment' was a numbered unit commanded by a Colonel, and a 'Battalion' was its tactical unit commanded by a Lt. Colonel. Nearly all regiments had only one battalion at this time.

On our arrival at Cananore we were Cantooned for the Winter, and weather permitting, constantly at Drill. Here we delivered up our Kings Arms and Appointments and received in exchange those of the Company which were shorter and considerably lighter. These on a march were a great ease to us, but what we gained by ease to our shoulders was often severely felt on the back, as the difference between the two firelocks often occasioned improper motions by the performer, which never past the eyes of (this son of Argus) our Commanding Officer (who was also a severe disciplinarian) without a smart caneing.

Here also we were new clothed and received a reinforcement of about 450 men from England raised as Independent Companies which again placed us on a respectable footing. The rains having ceased after a stay of about four months, we were again put in motion, and returned to our former Encampments on the Ghauts, where we were joined by some troops from Bengal among whom was the 73rd. Regiment, very strong.

After we had placed everything in readiness to proceed we awaited a short time for Orders from Marquis Cornwallis, who had now joined the Madras Army, and taken on him the Chief Command, which soon arrived and with it the 19th Light Dragoons and some Native Cavalry. We arrived safely at Seringapatam after six days marches during which we were daily annoyed by the Enemy without any material loss on our side or credit on theirs. On our arrival we took up our station about two miles East of the Madras Army and soon began constructing our Batterys for the Siege (which the Madras Army had already performed), but previous to our opening them the Enemy made a furious but unsuccessful sally from the Garrison, with his choicest Troops, on an advanced post of ours stationed in the Tope (Wood or pleasure shrubbery) under Command of Captn. M'Kenzie of the 75th. They were however repulsed with great loss, and had the party been permitted to follow would no doubt suceeded in taking the Garrison, as they could not have had time to shut the gates without Sacrifice of Thousands of his best men who would thereby have been prevented from entering.

The 75th lost one sergeant, two drummers and 13 privates on this day, the whole army losing 51 Europeans and 53 sepoys.

As WK indicates, this sortie by Tipu's troops on the 22 February 1792 was his last effort, and the next day he accepted Cornwallis's proposals for a treaty, sending him his two sons as hostages. This was the end of the Second Mysore War, but a further campaign would be needed finally to break the power of Hyder Ali's dynasty.

This short but gallant affray brought the Sultan to his sences, and in a short time a Capitulation was agreed on and signed, but as the Marquis well knew, by his conduct not only at Coimbatore but in many other Instances, that a Treaty with him would avail nothing without enforced afterwards by Arms, insisted on his delivering his two Sons as Hostiges. This at last with great reluctance was complied with and the Armys broke up to their different Stations, where we soon received our Donation or Gratuity, in two payments of Fifty Two Rupees each (or two shillings and three pence each Rupee) which was the first and fairest shared money I ever saw divided.

We are once more returned to Cananore for a short season, but soon received orders to proceed to Calicut, near the place we first conquered our Enemys, where we were conveyed on Men of War, and placed in comfortable temporary Barracks, on a beautiful plain about a mile from the Town where we remained some years without doing anything worth notice except the capture of the small and almost defenceless Garrison of Mahe, which was taken without any opposition from the French by six companies of the 75th and a few Seapoys, the whole under the Command of Captain M'Kenzie, who was also at that time in command of the Regiment, Captn. Craufurd having obtained permission to visit the Presidency for a few months.

WK notes, in the earliest letter home still surviving, written from Cannanore on 3 October 1792, that only thirty from his 110 strong draft were still alive after these first campaigns,

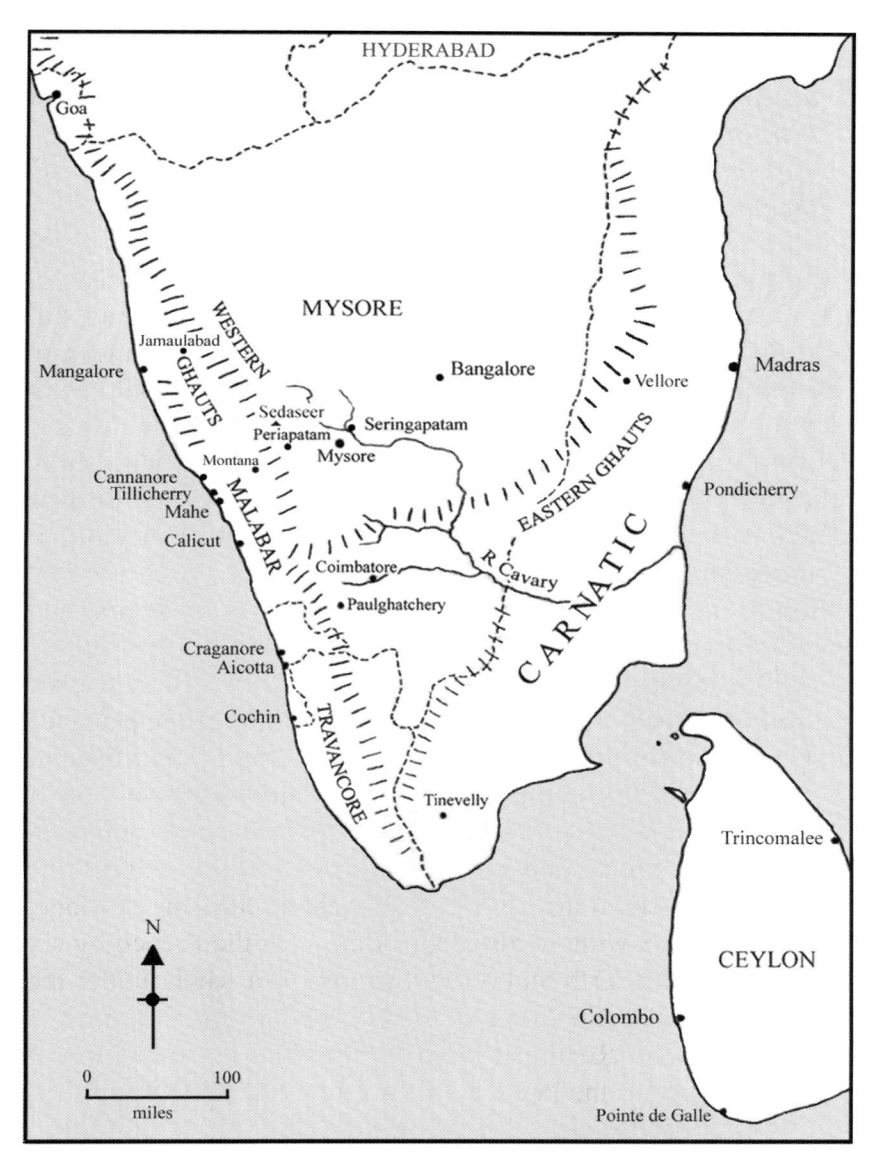

Southern India in the 1790's

and that disease rather than enemy action had accounted for most of the casualties.

About this time also Pondichery was taken from the French by the Madras Troops, under I believe General Brathwaite.

It is worth quoting from the story of Lachlan Macquarrie, later Governor of New South Wales, who was a captain in the 77th Regiment at the time.
"An Indian army of the eighteenth century on the march, isolated from its main bases by long stretches of wild land and sometimes wilder sea, necessarily must be self-sufficient or perish. Its leaders brought within their ambit every kind of available supply and transport facility, which assured the officer the comforts of home, the private soldier his domesticity, and the enemy the maximum degree of hostile attention.

Not merely was it necessary for Bombay's Commander to move three brigades of fighting men, equipped with artillery and siege trains, baggage trains and escorts. The private soldier went forth to war with all his prize possessions which he could carry or persuade someone else to carry. His officers braved the rigours of the Indian climate in capacious tents, six-ply and rainproof, furnished with elaborateness, equipped with stocks of wine and sometimes a lady, and transported and managed by menages which might have well been a source of envy to a travelling circus.

.... It was not abnormal to see forty servants in the retinue of an Indian Captain on campaign.

The native soldiery travelled equipped as comprehensively as the British. Every sepoy joined the ranks with his wife, his children, his bedstead, his cooking pots, his sacred cow or his goat, his pi-dogs and his poultry, and perchance even his grandfather and grandmother. Camp-followers swarmed and seethed in tens of thousands in the army's official bazaars, in *which named and ordered streets were moved forward as the army advanced and daily set down at each new camp in their original patterns.*

All trades followed the bazaars, the fortune teller and the silversmith, the horse-coper and the moneylender, the baker and the man with the dancing bear, the conjuror with his cobras, Phryne with her charms, Lazarus with his sores. All had their particular means of transport from Shanks's pony upwards, strange and makeshift by comparison with the immense official tide of pack-bullocks, at least three to a man, provided by the East India Company; puny beside the ponderous elephants, hired from large minded stock owners in Malabar, which hauled battering trains, siege equipment, and the eighteen pounders, which could be dragged along with their tumbrils......... only by sixty bullocks to a gun.

.... The aim was to rouse the men before daybreak, to have them on the road at six o'clock, to bring them into camp at noon before the full impact of the Indian midday heat had time to beat them down. But nature and the rains, hunger and mud, exhaustion of man and beast were alike elements in the game.

Sometimes they laboured from daylight to dusk to cover a few miles of hillside. Sometimes weary stragglers were still splashing into the disordered and tentless lines well into the darkness of the rain-drenched nights.

However, when circumstances allowed, the soldiers in their absurd three-cornered hats, their strangling neck-stocks, their long scarlet coats and their tight cross-belts, marched grimly along of a morning while the grease melted out of their pigtails and the sweat poured out of their tired, overloaded, fever-stricken bodies, to the intense satisfaction of illimitable hordes of Indian flies."

Chapter 3

The End of Tipu
1794 -1799

Shortly after this we received Orders to proceed to Craganore to be in readiness to assist the Dutch if necessary in the defence of Cochin, who were expecting a visit from the French. Here we remained till the rains commenced without any appearance of French and returned again to our old Station off Calicut, where we remained until 1796 without anything worth relating except quelling a few petty insuretions, and hanging the Authors of them.

In this city is a very well built but ancient Temple dedicated to an Ape, which is standing on a number of rich marble pillars. This place was some Years ago governed by its own Zamorin or Emperor, but when we conquered it 'twas in possession of Tippoo. The India Company have since retained it, as also all the whole of the fine Province of Malabar. It abounds in Cattle, Grain, Pepper and some Precious Stones.

Here are a number of Porcupines, Tigers, Jackals and other animals not common in Europe. We found good amusement in hunting the former. They are reckoned Delicious eating, but I never tasted any. It is said of this animal that he will defend himself gallantly till killed, by darting his quills at its enemy with great force even sufficient to pierce an Inch into a board. This I do not believe, But that they have power to dart their Quills which are very sharp, I admit, tho not with any degree of certainty in striking the object, and when frightened and agitated their attempts are very feeble indeed. They appear to be an Inoffensive and harmless animal.

The Jackal is called the Lyons Provider. If so, he has but little employ in those parts, there being no Lyons near it, and if there was I think they would be ill provided for, as this Animal itself is very voracious; their hours of prey would be insufficient to provide for themselves. We were always obliged to bury our dead at a great depth, and cover them thick with Bushes and Thorns to prevent them from tearing them up and devouring them.

Here our brave Commander Captn. Craufurd took leave of us for England, having previously made a considerable Promotion in the Non-Commissioned rank, to fill up vacancies, among which Number, I was appointed Corporal.

WK does not say when he was further promoted to Sergeant, but his discharge document says that he had held the rank for twenty years and nine months. As he was discharged on 25th January 1815, this would put this promotion about April 1794, so he was not a Corporal for long.

About the latter end of 1796 or begining of 97 we were relieved from the Coast Duty, much to our sorrow, by the 77th Regiment and replaced them in the Garrison of Bombay, where we remained till 1799, when we were again called on to visit our troublesome acquaintance Tippoo, but during the interval of our remaining in Bombay the 77th Regiment had taken Cochin, and had for a short time carried on an ineffectual war with the Rajah of Cotiote, which they for a season relinquished to join in opposing a more formidable enemy.

The Madras Army under Genl. Stuart had also made the captures of Columbo, Trincomallie and Jaffnapatam. The 36 & 52 Regt. then proceeded to England, and the 72nd. soon followed, from whom we received about 300 good volunteers.

The two flanks company of the 75 Regt. embarked about

the beginning of this Year, and the Battalion followed about a month after. Nothing worthy of observation passed till a few days before we joined them above Gauts in March, when the Army was Engaged with the greatest force the Enemy could spare for that purpose, but were completely foiled in the Attempt, and Obliged to retire to Seringapatam. This action took place near Sedasier (or Negroes Head) on the borders of Mysore.

> *This action at Sedaseer Hill, initially involving one brigade of Bombay native infantry, was very nearly a disaster, as Tipu managed to isolate the brigade and attacked it on all sides before being driven off by reinforcements, including the flank companies of the 75th.*

Shortly after joining, we proceeded on our March towards the Capital where we arrived about the begining of April, and took up our position on the opposite side of the river Cavary to which we before lay. The Madras Army on nearly the same Spot we occupied in 1792. General Harris had the Chief Command and under him Generals Baird and Wellesley. Genl. Stuart in Command of the Bombay Army.

> *Colonel Arthur Wellesley was the younger brother of the Governor General, and the future Duke of Wellington. He was not actually promoted Major-General until 1802.*

We immediately commenced throwing up our Works and in a short time both Batteries were completed, and opened on the Garrison with good effect.

A few evenings after our commencing the Bombardment, the enemy made an attempt to storm our Entrenchment, making his attack on different posts at the same time. I was that night on duty at the advance post under Colonel Mignan of the Companys Service. We received him in good order and maintained our post gallantly but with the loss of better than two thirds of our men killed or wounded, and had he at the end known our situation, he would not have hesitated to continue his attempt. We had not above thirty men fit to defend it, and the Ammunition nearly all spent, having only two rounds of Cannister for the Guns, and scarcely a round of Musquet shot. In this state he left us, and withdrew his men to Garrison. We were much better pleased with his absence than his Company.

In the morning we collected his dead which was very considerable, and no doubt they carried off a great many more. Had they not been sheltered by an old ruinous village their slaughter would have been much greater.

> *A force including the 75th had been ordered to attack and hold a small ruined village on the north bank of the river opposite the north western bastion of the fortress, so that guns could enfilade the enemy's entrenchments on the south side. A battery of six eighteen pounders was put in place, and caused the enemy to make great efforts to destroy them. This action took place on the 22nd April, and Fortescue records the loss of six or seven hundred of Tipu's men.*

After this attempt we remain.d pretty quiet and lost but a few men after, until the day of the storm, except now and then one or two by a chance shot in the trenches and at the relieving, when about the begining of May the breach was in great forwardness from the constant fireing of cross batteries for many days, and on the evening of the 3rd the storming party were lodged in the trenches under the Command of the brave General Baird. On the 4th exactly at 12 o'clock in the day, every man having taken his allowance of Arrack, the word was given by the brave Commander - "Tippoo - or no Baird. Follow me, my Lads, and we'll soon shave him." (To shave a Mahometan is the greatest insult you can offer him. Genl. Baird was determined, had he taken him alive, to have had him shaved for the ill treatment he had experienced from him when prisoner.)

The then Captain Baird had been severely wounded and captured at the Battle of Pollilur by Tipu and his father Hyder Ali in 1780, when the Madras Army had been almost annihilated. He then endured nearly four years of ill treatment in chains as Tipu's prisoner in Seringapatam. Not unnaturally, he was bent on revenge.

Only the flank companies of the 75th took part in the final assault. It is probable that WK was with one of the battalion companies manning the trenches on the far side of the Cavary River, and thus was not a direct eyewitness of the storming of the breach. However, his version of Baird's words before the assault rings truer than the rather more conventional sayings attributed to him by later biographers.

The Forlorn Hope under Sergt. Graham of the Companys service immediately rushed on followed by the Covering Party and main body, when a tremendous firing commenced from different quarters of the Garrison, with considerable effect on our troops in passing the Cavary river. Yet undismayed, the survivors of the Forlorn Hope mounted the breech and planted the British Colour, and when in the act of cheering, the brave Serjeant fell. Colonel Dunlop of the 77th here received a severe but happily not Fatal Sabre wound. Having gained a footing in the Garrison, the Enemy after defending each post till driven from them by the point of the Bayonet, the party divided itself right and left and soon scoured the whole ramparts and fortified places to the very palace where the Tyrant was expected to be found, but he was withdrawn, leaving his sons who knew not where their Father was. He was however, before this, most probably slain. His body was found among a heap of Dead, endeavouring it was supposed to prevent his men from deserting, or perhaps with the design of making his own escape, but from the crowd collected at this one spot, which was only a sally port, numbers were shot & fell by the Bayonet, and many more trampled to death. By whom he was slain no one knows, tho many claim the honor. I can say with

Shakesperes Macbeath "Shake not thy Hoary Locks at me, thou canst not say 'I did it'." Previous to the storm commencing, he had ordered the whole of the Garrison Gates to be closed, which prevented many hundreds not bearing arms from escaping, by which rash and Cruel Order he not only lost his own life, but that of nearly the whole of his Garrison. As in this short but fortunate affray not only men but Women and children were slain (not by the British) but by the Seapoys, who were so exasperated that it was with difficulty their Officers could prevent a total extirpation of both sexes.

    Thus, in about two hours, fell the greatest and most powerful of the Indian Monarchs. The British Flag flying, and his Concubines, Wives & Children Captives. The former to be protected and the latter close prisoners, and as such were marched to Vellore Garrison, where for anything I know they now remain, but with considerable liberty, Princely attendance and Maintainence.

    A good plunder was made by some (altho prohibited) on this occasion and many could not get anything; those however who made the most, were little better than those who got nothing in a few days or months at farthest. One poor fellow of the 75th named Rider, having made a good booty, soon drank his sences away, and Judas like, went out and hanged himself. This is all can be expected from Ill gotten wealth.

> *In a letter to his mother, Colonel Wellesley wrote -*
> "Nothing therefore can have exceeded what was done on the night of the 4th. Scarcely a house in the town was left unplundered, and I understand that in camp jewels of the greatest value, bars of gold, etc. etc., have been offered for sale by our soldiers, sepoys and followers. I came in to take command on the morning of the 5th and by the greatest exertion, by hanging, flogging etc., etc., in the course of that day I restored order among the troops, and I hope I have gained the confidence of the people. They are returning to

their houses and beginning again to follow their occupations, but the property of everyone is gone."

On the following Evening the remains of the Tyrant were removed to the Burial Place of his Father and interd. in a Tomb close to old Hider Ally, in the Lollbang Gardens. Minute Guns were fired during the Ceremony, I think there was sixty two, being the number of his Years, but cannot positively say.

After his interment the most awful storm of Hail, Thunder and Lightning I ever saw or heard of came on and continued for a long time, the dreadful effect of which were felt on both man and beast; several men were killed among whom was Lieut. Grant of the 77th. The greatest part of our Draught Cattle perished, and much of the Tents and Camp Equipage destroyed.

A few days after this we proceeded to Canniamhadie (about twelve miles) where we remained till arrangements were made by the Commander in Chief for the protection of the Province. The 12th, 33rd and Scotch Brigade now 94th Regt. remained in Garrison with some Battalions of Seapoys.

Here we were joined by the Division of the Army under Colonel Brown, among whom was five Companies of the 19th Foot. They were fortunate enough to partake of their small share of Prize money, being 18 Star Pagodas which at 8s 6d each is £7. 13.0.

In 1792 under Marquis Cornwallis the Donation of each was £11.14.0. but there was no one eight of the whole to an Individual, no twelve Hundred Shares to others and so on to reduce it.

How the Prize Agents acted in this business - God only knows, and not I. Honestly though, no doubt, being all Gentlemen of high Military Rank.

It would be cruel and disrespectful to suppose Gentlemen of the Sword, Sash and Gorget would behave any way dishonest. What if they did remove a few Tons of Elephants Teeth (Vulgarly called Ivory) to bring the sale to a more speedy conclusion, did we not the sooner receive our Prize. Or what if they did Pocket a few white or Yellow Pebbles did that not also forward the business and lastly those trinkets formed something like a round O and a paltry pebble pasted, Glued, or Hammered on it, was that anything to us whether they were sold or not, we received our Prize money, and like good Soldiers ought to be thankfull.

    I will not take upon myself however to vindicate the conduct of some of the Clerks not being Gentlemen. And this I am well convinced of. A poor simple Honest Scotsman, then a Corporal and Acting Serjeant in the 75th brought home money enough (after being a clerk to one of them) to purchase sufficient ointment to destroy the Itch from every Inhabitant of that large and populous city called Aberdeen, and of which City both himself and employer were Natives. Another apology and I shall not endeavour further to vindicate the conduct of our brave officers. There is an old Loyal and Warlike song The Chorus to which is – "For Britons never shall be Slaves"- this song no doubt our gallant officers had often heard sung and it seemed to ring with double violence in their ears after the firing of Cannon and Musquitry had ceased for immediate orders were given to our Regt. to abstain from plunder, and some who had got a trifle were robbed of it by the Agents, For why: because they had gotten a few gold chains and bangles which those worthy Gentlemen could not bear to behold. No doubt shuddering with the Idea of seeing their countrymen loaded with Chains; an appearance so derogatory to the nature of a Briton.

    The plunder of Seringapatam by those who were fortunate enough to conceal it caused much and constant Gambling in Camp night and day, which before we were strangers to. I have seen Fifteen, Sixteen and sometimes Twenty Europeans and Natives in a Game of Chance for each a handful of Untold Gold, the highest Dice swept the whole, some have continued at this until rendered unfit Companies to associate any longer with them by a failure in trade, but as borrowing and lending was prohibitted, very few Bankrupcys followed, and as there were

Seringapatam 1799

also several Gambling tables on a more limited scale, they might accomodate themselves in a small way elsewhere. This continued three or four months, when with the exception of what in cloths, Bangles and Rings etc. with what they had ornamented their Black comrades and bosom friends, and that which was in the hands of the Brandy and Wine Merchants, the camp again became as thin of Money as was the camp of the Lord Protector Cromwell previous to his Engagement with the Royal Army of King Charles. The Natives, who were by far the most expert in the Art, carried away in the end the greater part of this rich Booty. The last resource was the Dis-robeing and Un-Jewelling their Ladies which most frequently ended in a divorse. The unfortunate Damsels thus stript generally soon after began packing up her Sifting articles, Grinding Stones, and Cooking Pots, and if she had any children, them she left with her husband as a remembrance of Past love. All things being thus arranged she Decamps to provide herself a more fortunate Husband. The parting farewell was in general accompanied with a heavy, and sometimes Prophetic Malediction.

> *Prize money and its allocation was a main preoccupation of a soldier's life, as it was one of the few ways he could improve his lot. Entitlements to prize shares were often traded and willed to friends, as WK notes years later in one of his letters back in England, but payments frequently took years to materialise. The system was of course heavily biased towards rank and seniority, and open to fraud on a huge scale. The 'official' prize money from Seringapatam was £1,143,216, a vast sum for the time, but probably an even vaster sum disappeared as plunder before the Prize Agents started work. The East India Company bickered about prize money with the senior army officers for years afterwards. WK, who as a pay sergeant was in a position to know what was going on, is scathing.*

We returned after a few Weeks towards the Malabar Coast, but did not remain anytime settled till arrival at Mangalore the Capital of the Province of Cannara, the Kelledar of which having been informed of the fall of Seringapatam and fate of his Master, did not hesitate to deliver up that place to Col. Montresor, who was then Our Commander. Resistance would have been vain as the Fort (if so it may be called) was a heap of ruins, and nearly defenceless in men and ammunition. The Kelledar of Jemaulabad a Hill Fort about thirty miles East of Mangalore was more obstinate and with a better prospect of success, having a Garrison to defend which defied the skill and bravery of man. Situate on almost a Perpendicular Hill, any attempt to expugn them was rashness and folly, but which was in vain attempted twice or thrice.

Had they not a musquet or Gun in their possession (but both of which they were well supplied with) we never could have effected it, as the only passage to it was by a stair case from the Top of which they might roll stones of some Tons Weight which would carry and sweep all before it.

Our Guns or Mortars were useless, as they could not be sufficiently elevated to throw Shot or Shell near them. Thus circumstanced we remained some weeks, till the Kelledar fearful his Obstinancy would be attended with fatal concequences, and perhaps in the end suffer the worst of Deaths, Starvation, sent proposals to give it up, which was gladly excepted, and the defenders allowed to proceed where they pleased. Thus ended the Mysore War on our part, and shortly after with the other Armys Sevendrooy, Numdedrooy, Onore, Bedanore, and all the other Garrisons surrendered to the Madras Army as they advanced to receive them and the War thus begun in 1799, was in less than a twelvemonth completely ended.

The capture of Seringapatam and the death of Tipu Sultan captured the imagination of the British public, and was commemorated in pictures and pageants for many years afterwards. Even J.M.W. Turner painted a watercolour of the defences of the fortress, based on eye witness's sketches. A large amount of booty returned to England, the most famous item being Tipu's automaton of a tiger savaging an european soldier, which is now in the Victoria and Albert Museum.

Chapter 4

The Pacification of the South
1800 - 1802

We had now a short respite, and received our Prize money, but before a few months had expired Jemaulabad was retaken and in possesion of Rebels, and in fact the most part of this province was in a state of Rebellion. The manner etc. of their getting possesion of this unlucky Garrison was nearly as follows.

A considerable number of Recruits from the late Sultains Army had entered in our Seapoy Battalions. An Officer also of low rank named Tim Naig entered into the Grenadier Battn. with the rank of Havaldar (Serjeant) and in consideration of his bringing over a number of fine recruits to accompany him was promised afterwards to be promoted to Jemadar (Ensign) but having continued some time at Drill, and despairing of his promise ever being verefied formed the desperate and horrid design of not only deserting himself and taking a number of the Battalion with him, but seizing and putting to death all the party on duty at Jemaulabad, which was executed by a few of his men gaining Admittance as Show Men or Jugglers.

The Detachment of Seapoys were commanded by a Young Officer, who had a Native Woman to his Companion, and by her he was informed of the danger to which he was exposing himself and Men. Unfortunately it being about Midday, the greater part of his men were from the Garrison and the Officer regardless of his informers advice, was indulging himself with their Antic performance until the remainder rushed in and put them all to death and threw their bodies over the Wall where they became food for the Jackal below. This done they immediately put the Fort in the best manner of defence they were able and having in the Neighbourhood collected a good supply of Grain thought themselves secure.

It was some days before *[news of]* this Tragic affair reached us, but when it did a Party was immediately ordered to proceed and retake it, altho in the middle of the Monsoons, and for the last few days the rain had fallen so heavy and the rivers were so much swoln as not to be fordable, a considerable delay therefore unavoidably followed, which gave the rebels a short respite, during which they were not Idle nor negligent in putting themselves in the best possible state to receive us.

The rains having abated and the rivers becoming fordable the Detachment arrived and summoned them to surrender at discretion but this you may be sure they knew their case would not Admit of, and altho but a few men experienced told us from a former Occasion any attempt to storm it would be folly, as their mode of defence was similar to that carryed on by the former defenders of it, and indeed there were some who had before served at its defence. The Commanding Officer therefore was Obliged to carry on a protracted state of Warfare in order to starve or bring them to submission on our own terms. This, after about two months blockading had the desired effects, their provision being all expended, the greater part had formed the design of escaping by lowering themselves down by ropes and thus descending the rocks, but in this desperate attempt they nearly all perished. I believe two or three succeded in it, the others who attempted it were dashed to Atoms in the fall.

Those who submitted to Mercy were brought back to Mangalore and shortly after tried by a court martial and hanged.

The Ringleader of this Murderous event was taken and after trial was blown from a Gun. He met his fate in a very unconcerned manner.

About this time numbers were brought in from different Quarters of the Province, so soon the flames of Rebellion spread, and had it not been immediately extinguished and punished by severe and summary examples, God only knows what might have been the Consequence.

The Province being thus declared in a state of Rebellion, a Native General Court Martial followed. Shake Shabidar Tollerker, a Subadar in the Grenadier Battn. and the Senior Native Officer of that Presidency was appointed President and a more severe President never Adjudged man. He was the Jeffries of India. Thirty and upwards have been tried and convicted by him in less than that number of Minutes. And for many weeks scarce a day passed but executions took place.

I have seen twenty and upwards executed on one Gallows, and never saw a man who feared Death or appeared anyway dejected. They generally in the Morning previous to execution eat an uncommon hearty breakfast of Boiled Rice and some would carry a part with them and Continue eating till under the Gallows, and the Ropes round their necks. What remained was the only fees the Executioner (general an Halalcore) might expect. Cloths they scarcely had enough to cover their nakedness.

One Morning the Provost Serjeant on calling over the names of his Prisoners for Execution found one missing and was Informed by the other prisoners that he had the day before been released by himself thro a Mistake in the Name (many of which bear a strong resemblance in pronunciation) but the Serjeant was not to be deprived of his fees, and probably Office, through an oversight, and with an oath declared he'd be D---d. if he cared, he would carry out his number and accordingly took the first man that came to hand, who happened to be a poor fellow who was confined for a petty offence but who did not hesitate to comply with the Order, and when the names were called over under the Gallows he answered to the name of the Absentee and suffered accordingly.

This is a most beautiful province and rich in every article of

Life. Considerable Manufactorys of Cloth etc. are now established and has a good Seaport, but the greatest evil attending the country is a small destructive Insect called the White Ant. This little animal is about the size and somewhat the appearance of a body louse, they associate and commit their depradations in Armys, as the Common Ant. They will sometimes destroy in the course of a night the whole of a soldiers Knap-sack and contents. Blankets and Cloth are their favourite food, nor is wood refused by them. Our Barracks in the course of a Winter were generally so much destroyed by them as to be useless and obliged to be Annualy rebuilt.

It is said also that Iron will not resist their ravages. Previous to our arrival in India a circumstance had occured in the Ordnance Department, and as we were Informed, as well as I can remember was as follows.

A few Iron Eighteen pounders were missing from the Garrison of Tillichery and the Conducter having been questioned concerning them could only Account for the deffeciency as having been devoured by this mischevious Insect. This however was not considered a sufficient explanation by the Chief Officer of that department, and he being somewhat subject to the failing of unbelief declared it impossible. An Investigation of the affair took place, and which was succeeded by a General Court Martial, but nothing aspired or transpired to bring the mistery to light. He was acquited of Embezzlement, but dismissed for Neglect.

About the beginning of this Year, six Compys, of the Regt. were ordered to proceed to the Malabar Coast. The Rajah of Cotiote still continuing his depradations on the Company subjects, war was declared and the Command of this service given to Lt. Col. Cumine of the 75th. The forces consisted of detachments from many Regiments of Seapoys together with a Battn of Pioneers raised for the service and a Company of Artillery.

We were landed at Tillechery and two days marches brought us into the Enemys Country, which altho of great extent begins and ends in a thick jungle or wood. Our first attempt was the relief of Montana distant about Thirty miles. A Company of Seapoys had penetrated thus far up when they were surrounded, but found an opportunity to make their situation known to Our Commander by means of a Spy, and afterwards bravely defended themselves until Our Arrival which from the many obsticles thrown in our way was better than a fortnight.

This War was carried on in a way very different to any we had yet been engaged in. From the moment we left Cotiparambo, which is only eight miles from Tillichery, the Capital of British Malabar, we were annoyed by numerous unseen Enemys. The thick Bamboo bushes and Trees Shrubbs etc. afforded them a commodious and safe retreat and to add to this the road was rendered totally unpassable by their felling Trees of immense size across it, through which we were necessitated to wait and assist the Pioneers in removing, during this we were sure to be saluted with a volley of Arrows, but the greatest vexation was not to see from whence or from whom they came, by this means we had many killed and wounded. I received one in my left knee on one of those occasions, but It was not attended with any bad concequences. At last our Commanding Officer fell on the resolve of street firing which had the desired effect of being no more troubled with them in that way, but it cost a great quantity of ammunition.

'Street Firing' was a standard but little used drill manoeuvre intended, as the name implies, for use when a column was advancing down a street with enemy on either side. It involved the front ranks of the leading company subsection, turning right and left respectively and firing their muskets into the jungle on each side of the road. Having fired, the men would then march by files down each side of the column to the rear, reload, and reform. The next ranks would move forward and do the same, so that an almost continuous fire was kept up as the column advanced. In the circumstances,

this could only be carried out successfully for any distance by very well drilled troops, and, as WK notes, expended large amounts of ammunition.

Captain Macquarie of the 77th, writing at the end of this campaign, describes the Pyche Rajah's troops -
'[they] must now be fully sensible that they never can stand against us in the field, even in their own extraordinary mode of warfare and monkey-like way of fighting from the tops of trees! - It is true we cannot say to a certainty we have killed many of them in this last service .....[Their dead] are instantly carried off the moment they fall. - But we may judge from the dreadful yells and screams of the enemy every time our troops fired at them into the jungle, tho' generally at random, there must have been a considerable number of them killed and wounded on this last service.'

We had not however, proceeded a great way till new Obstacles presented themselves. Many Stockade and Batterys were thrown up by the Enemy and were deffended with Wall Pieces and matchlocks, and a bold but savage band of soldiers, who would seldom fly, but rather suffer death than quit the post they were instructed to defend.

We however, at last succeded and arrived at Monthana, but the small Army was in a very diminished state, having exclusive of the killed, wounded and sick been much weakened by leaving small detachments at each fort after getting possession of them. This being done, we for months were traversing this wild and barbarous looking country without any effect. When we were in the one part, the Rajah and his men were in the other, we however continued marching and countermarching till the rains commenced and drove us to Montana when we Cantooned for the Winter, having only taken one Fort called Pychee and fought nearly twenty actions with generally an Invisible Enemy. During the Monsoons we were left very quiet and had but little to do. Indeed we had scarcely anybody to do that little, but before the spring received a reinforcement from the Regiment still at Mangalore, together with new Clothing which we were in great need of as the thick and sharp bushes had left us literally naked.

> *WK wrote from Montana on 24 September 1801, with a long and quite detailed account of what he was up to at the time. See letter 2.*

As we had now a fair open road during the Winter we were well supplied with every requisite from Tillechery and upon the whole passed as comfortable a Winter as ever I did at any time during my residence in India.

We opened our next Campaign with similar Manouvres to the former, but without any effect, no Rajah could be found, nor heard of. His followers appeared also to have vanished and many houses we before passed uninhabited were again peopled, having undoubtedly fled from his Service and returned to their homes.

Proclamations were soon after issued assuring protection and forgiving all past to those who would return, which they mostly all did, and which had the effect in a very short time of restoring peace in the Cotiote.

Great rewards were offered to those who would give information of the Rajahs retreat but without effect, and we shortly after left them and proceeded on another route to other parts of India.

Thus ended a War of about 18 months duration and during which we had scarcely ever seen the sun being in a manner Eclipsed by a thick Jungle.

> *The pacification of Southern India, involving relatively small numbers of British troops, was one of those arduous campaigns which, while not attracting much attention, was vital in the scheme of things. At this time these insurrections could easily have escalated into significant diversions from*

the more well known campaigns in Egypt and Europe, at a point in history when Britain was at great risk from Napoleon.

This Wild Country is of great value in concequence of the quantity of fine Pepper produced in it which is so abundant that scarcely a tree standing but is Incircled with a vine of it in resemblance something like Ivy - The Pepper growing in Clusters as bunches of Grapes, and did not here appear to have been anything assisted by Art Or Manual Labour and Cultivation.

This Country also produces abundance of Game such as Ducks, Peacocks, Pigeons, Hares, and vast numbers of Monkeys or Baboons are seated and apparently in close conversation or debate on the trees above you, and it requires a person to have his eyes about him travelling as they would frequently break off a rotten bough from the tree of considerable weight and drop it on a careless passenger. The Amazing leaps they make from tree to tree is astonishing, altho they are frequently incumbred with a young one hanging by the Feet to the Mother or properly speaking hanging by its hands and feet round the Parents body, but with it they will spring some yards.

The Peacocks are most beautiful, and are partly in a wild state and partly Domesticated, being fed and protected through the day by the Inhabitants from whom they receive adoration, at night they return to the woods. They are dry eating but well enough tasted to a hungry man. In those parts as also the whole of Malabar are numbers of what they call the Flying Fox. They are something of the Bat kind, webfooted and very sharp claws, large sinewey wings and bodies covered with a fine dark brown Fur. They subsist on vermin, which they provide themselves with at night being as the Owl not able to desern objects after sun rise. They are about the size of a small Rabbit but when flying appear a great deal larger. In the mornings after day break they retire home to their place of rest for the day, which is always in the same place, they take their repose in a seeming painful manner, which is by hanging with their claws to the Boughs of trees. The Head and body extended downward in this posture they remain till evening except disturbed by the report of a Gun of some other great noise, when they all together make off and if by chance a tree falls in their way they reassemble and resume their ordinary repose.

It is not uncommon on the sea coast during the Monsoons to see it rain fish, but of a small size. I have seen many drop about three or four inches in length something resembling a sprat and full of life for some time after. They are as I suppose caught up by what the Mariners call a Water Spout.

Fish of various kinds are abundantly supplied here, not only from the sea but the many rivers watering the Province which is a great nourishment to many casts of Natives who are forbidden by the laws and customs of their ancestors and religion to eat Animal Food.

Here are also a number of Droves of the Buffalo kind which they herd for the purpose of Milk and Butter, their flesh is far inferior to the Ox, but we were often obliged and glad to get it when the other could not be procured. They are said to be amphibious but if so the Native Indians are the same, as they are generally in the water the greater part of the day, but not under water for any length of time, nor is the Buffalo as ever I saw.

The Fruit also is very abundant but the best is the Plaintain, Banana, PineApple, Mango and Guava, each of which are most delicious and considered wholesome if not eaten to excess.

The Vegetables are many unknown in England, and also many that are here common, such as Onions, Cabbages and Potatoes of many sorts, the Onions run of a great size but more cold and perfectly white. Here is also plenty of fine Yams which I allways prefered to their Potatoes.

Sugar cane is cultivated in some parts of this Province as is also Tobacco but in no great abundance, but both of which are good of their kind, though not by any means equal to that of the West India produce. About the middle of this year the principle part of the Forces were withdrawn from Cotiote. We proceeded to Tillechery and soon after Embarked on coasting vessels of the Arabs for Goa, a settlement of the Queen of Portugal where the remainder of Our Regt and the 84th lay under command of Colonel Sir Wm Clarke to whom the Portuguese Government had transfered the Command. We did not land here, but remained a few days till more suitable vessels were provided to convey us, which being done we removed and made the best of Our way to the Presidency, which we made in about ten days.

Goa is a fine settlement and abundantly supplied with the necessarys of life, but as all Romish settlement it is eaten up by their Bigoted Clergy. Their Priests, Friars, Monks, Jesuits etc. having converted numbers of the lowest orders of the People from Paganism to Idolatry, they live therefore on the Fat of the land. But it is a doubt which can only be solved by the Divine which of the two is preferable, and which in the eyes of an Impartial and just God will be found most exceptable in the days of Judgement. For my part must say the former, if their natural simplicity and Ignorance may be admitted in excuse. But the latter altho nearly equal in Ignorance to the former in matters of religion, cannot but be sensible that they are leading them astray to enrich their own bodies at the expence of those poor wretched souls, who would, I am fully convinced if properly Instructed, become not only good Christians, but an honour to their Instructors and the profession.

Chapter 5

A Change of Scene
1802 - 1803

On our arrival at Bombay we disembarked hoping to enjoy a short repose, short indeed it proved, for in less than a month we were again on board and landed in Cambay in the Province of Guzerat, here we joined Detachments of the 88th, 86th and Companies European Regt with a Battalion of Surat Seapoys and part of the Bombay Marine Battalion, the whole under Command of Major Walker of the Companys Service. This small Division being in want of every requisite to equip it for the Field, was detained here some weeks during which we were joined by a small Irregular Army of Natives under Command of Amier Cawn, a petty Prince whose Country borders on ours at Surat, and with whom after being supplied with what was necessary, proceeded on our march towards Kurria, the Rajah of which had been subordinate to the Guicore Rajah, but became refractory and had taken the Field against him with such success that he was obliged to apply to the English Government for assistance which they are allways ready and willing to afford to any one desiring it.

Amier Cawn is probably Amir Khan, a close associate of Holkar. The "Guicore Rajah" is the Gaekwar of Baroda, a Mahratta chief who later opposed the British.

Nothing worth notice occured on the March till our arrival

there except passing the large and populous city of Amedabad, the walls of which are of great height, and numbers of small Towers defended with Wall Pieces. This is the Capital of the Province and the largest City I ever saw. The walls are said to be twenty miles in circumference but slightly built, and I think a very few shots would soon lay them flat enough, but this was not our business to attempt. It was taken a few years before my arrival in India by a small Army of the British under Gen Goddard, but restored soon after.

Several of the soldiers who had served at its defence came to our Camp, some without legs and some without arms, asking Charity. This city is about 400 miles to the Northward of Bombay, standing on the banks of a small Navigable river, for vessels of a small size to Cambay. The river swarms with fish, and harbours great quantitys of Wild Fowl, nearly all the year round.

We arrived at Kurria on St. Patricks day and encamped within Gun shot of the Fort, the Rajah having withdrawn his Troops close under the walls. Our Commander immediately sent Captain Williamson, his Acting Brigade Major to the Garrison with a flag, but he did not, I believe, like his message as he was not permitted to return and immediately commenced firing on our lines, which obliged us to fall back and form Line. His Troops also did the same and in about half an hour after, both Armys engaged, but from the carnage made on our Troops from the Guns of the Garrison, the Commander thought proper to retire without effecting anything except the killing a few of his men, but we lost a great many more than him in concequence of the great disadvantage to which we were exposed from the Grape and Round shot of the Guns from his Garrison. Our Field Pieces were in a very short space of time dismounted and the best of the Draught Cattle slain. Our small Detachment was also much diminished and thus we left them for that time and retired to Camp, which we entrenched to defend ourselves (should he attempt to attack us) until a reinforcement arrived to our

Assistance from Bombay.

We lost One Captain, Three Lieutenants and about 150 Men in this affair, and a great many more wounded.

The Rajah made some attempts but without success of carrying our lines, and finding he could do no good, afterwards contented himself with the Fortifying his Garrison and throwing out works, rightly guessing we had not entirely dropt the business, and after a short time our reinforcement arrived under Command of Colonel Sir Wm Clarke having the remainder of the 75th, and 84th Regt with three Battalions of seapoys.

The Conducting of the Rajahs business was entrusted to an Englishman named Parker who was both Engineer and Commandant, how he came into his service or what he had been, we never could learn, but most probably had been an Officer in the Company Service and Cashiered, be it what it may he was everything but a Coward and Fool, which he convinced us he was not.

I shall just note a circumstance that occured on the day of our arrival here. Two men of the Company to which I belonged named Dixon and Finnukin, having carried a Sheeps head with them to refresh with on the road, they sat down (during a short halt) for that purpose and having eaten all the meat began throwing the Brains at each other when Dixon made an ominus remark desiring his Comrade to desist, saying that very probably their own brains might be flying about in a similar manner before night. This actually happened. Dixon during the Action was placed in the front rank, and covered by Finnukin. A Cannon shot from the Garrison came and struck off both their heads, and their brains as Dixon had hinted, were plentifully strewed in the faces of myself and another Serjeant in the rear of the Company near where these two unfortunate men fell.

Colonel Sir William Clark having joined and taken the Command, immediate preparation was made to attempt an Escalade on the Garrison, should we fail in blowing open the Gates.

The next morning, about two o'clock the whole Line was under Arms for this purpose. We had not above two miles to march, had we gone in a strait direction, but this was not considered advisable, but took a Circuitous direction to avoid his Picquets and Out-Posts, who would have immediately given the Alarm, had we fallen in with them. It was therefore, just on the break of day before we arrived at the first of his Defences, which was a small Tower and a Six Gun battery, thrown up by Parker during the time we lay before the Garrison. Their Guns being allready loaded with Grape Shot, on our approach was discharged but with little effect as they were taken by surprise they had not time to level them, and the Grenadier Company of the 75th headed by Col Clark rushed in and took possession. This gave the Alarm to the Garrison which was within an Hundred Yards of it and who immediately commenced a heavy fire on it, which caused the Col. to order the spikeing of the Guns, and after destroying as much as time would admit of the party, left it and joined us who had by this time got possession of the whole of his Out-Posts and a small Town (called Pettah). And now our Artillery commenced throwing shells into the Fort with such Effect that the Rajah was obliged to ask Mercy, which was granted on condition of his throwing open the Gates and admitting the British Troops into Garrison. The 75th and a Battalion of Seapoys then entered, but everything being settled to the satisfaction of Our Commander, the Troops were withdrawn to Camp the same night, and all quiet.

In saying all was quiet, I tell a falsehood, for an accident of an unpleasant nature happened just after our Arrival.

After being Dismissed and the Arms and Colours piled, a Sentinel from the 84th Regt who was on duty on the left flank of their Regiment, through Ignorance or God knows what else, fired a shot past our double sentries at the Centre. This they returned and in a moment the whole Camp was in an Alarm, and did not end until one of the 75th was killed. The 84th Sentry was confined, but I never heard of any enquiry ever being made into the business.

As this was not considered as a Capture, Plunder was not admitted, but several made well enough by it for all that, and I myself could not avoid taking up a few Yards of rich Embroidery that lay in my way, which I brought off and sold for about fifty-shillings English, but had I dared to have exposed it to sale I doubt not it was worth Fifteen Pounds, which I might have had at a fair sale for it.

A Comrade Serjeant of mine named Pat Kennedy who accompanied me on this marauding business was far less fortunate than myself, for having passed a small Brass Foundry, where the Rajah had been Casting Metal Cannon, nothing could persuade Paddy but the melted drops was pure Gold, he accordingly packed up about 30 Pounds Weight of it into his Knapsack. And being fearfull from the strict order regarding plunder, to offer it for sale in Camp laboured under it until arrival at Cambay about 150 miles, here he thought he might without danger venture to turn it into Rupees, but to his great astonishment was informed that it was not worth a Farthing. It was long however before he could be brought to believe this, but after hawking it about from place to place and nearly laughed out of his Irish sences, got fairly tired of it, and at last was persuaded to throw it into the sea.

But this was not all the Misfortune attending my Comrade, for being at first fully satisfied he could turn his valuable plunder into cash at any time after arrival in Cambay had thrown the whole of his necessary (except the cloths on his back) away to make room for his darling Gold, and in a small degree to ease his shoulders of the great weight to which between them both he must have been exposed. All these articles was poor Patrick obliged to replace before he could properly appear on a clean dressd. Parade.

A Battalion of Seapoys being left at Kurria to enforse (Mathar Row) the Rajahs compliance with the terms granted him, the remainder marched back to the Coast, and the rains

1. The Uniform of the 75th Highland Regiment on formation in 1787.
On arrival in India, the kilt and bonnet were abandoned
for white cotton trousers and a round black hat.

2. An East-Indiaman, similar to the Ponsborne, off the Cape of Good Hope in 1790.

3. A Contemporary print of General Baird leading the assault on Seringapatam.

MAJOR-GENERAL ROBERT CRAUFURD,
Leader of the Light Division.

4. General Robert Crauford, from a portrait bust commissioned after he became well known during the Peninsular War.

5. A sergeant of the 75th Highlanders about 1799 in Southern India

SIR DAVID BAIRD DISCOVERING THE BODY OF TIPPOO SAIB

6. A Victorian engraving of the death of Tipu, illustrating the common misconception by home based artists that Highland Regiments wore the kilt in India at that time.

7. This romanticised portrait of General Baird was painted after he lost an arm at Corunna.

8. This cartoon was published in September 1809, while the unfortunate remnants of the Expedition were still in Walcheren.

9. Soon after this picture was taken in 1931, Moon's Farm suffered a serious fire, and was rebuilt in it's current form.

> **Sacred**
> To the Memory of
> WILLIAM KENWARD
> late Pay Master Sergeant
> in the 76 Regiment of Foot
> He served in various Regiments
> of the Line upwards of 30 years
> and was of late years
> A CHELSEA PENSIONER
> who died at Lewes May 6 1828
> Aged 61 Years

10. William Kenward's gravestone in Fletching Churchyard is in the centre of the picture, at the end of a row of Kenward tombs. The inscription is now barely legible.

1801 for many Weeks scarce a day passed but
Executions took place —
I have seen twenty and upwards Executed on
One Gallows, and never saw a man who
feared Death, or appeared any way dejected
they generally in the Morning previous
to execution eat an uncommon hearty
breakfast of Boiled Rice, and some would
Carry a part with them and Continue eat
-ing till under the Gallows, and the Rope
round their Necks. What remained was the
Only fees the Executioner (general an Dalelcoey)
might expect Cloths they scarcely had
Enough to cover their Nakedness —
One Morning the Provost Serjeant on call
-ing over the names of his Prisoners for
Execution found one missing, and was In
formed by the other prisoners that he had
the day before been Released by himself thro
a Mistake in the Name (many of which

11. The memoirs were written in a clear copperplate hand typical of an experienced army clerk. William Kenward's earliest letter from India is noticeably less well written.

The Kenward Family in Newick and Fletching

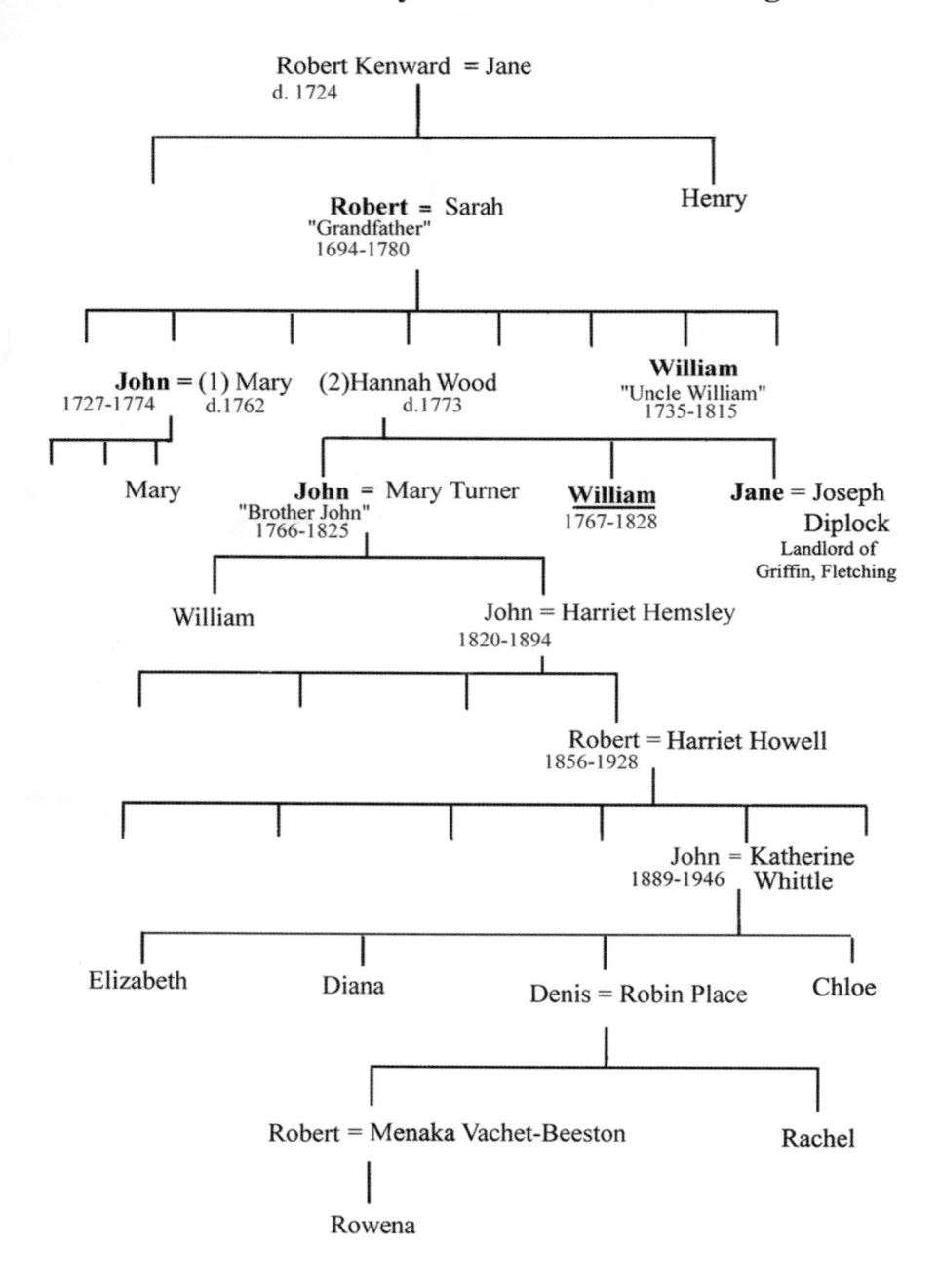

- Robert Kenward (d. 1724) = Jane
  - **Robert** "Grandfather" (1694-1780) = Sarah
    - **John** (1727-1774) = (1) Mary (d.1762); (2) Hannah Wood (d.1773)
      - Mary (from first marriage)
      - **John** "Brother John" (1766-1825) = Mary Turner
        - William
        - John (1820-1894) = Harriet Hemsley
          - Robert (1856-1928) = Harriet Howell
            - John (1889-1946) = Katherine Whittle
              - Elizabeth
              - Diana
              - Denis = Robin Place
                - Robert = Menaka Vachet-Beeston
                  - Rowena
                - Rachel
              - Chloe
      - **William** (1767-1828)
      - **Jane** = Joseph Diplock, Landlord of Griffin, Fletching
    - **William** "Uncle William" (1735-1815)
  - Henry

having commenced our Regt took up its quarters in Cambay, the remainder of the Army proceeded to Surat and Bombay. We had our Barracks to build, but assisted in both men and materials by the English Resident officiating as Consol, this Gentlemans name was Holford, who thro a long habit of the Mahomedan Customs had all the outward appearance of being such, but his Heart was truly Christian. His Generosity to our Regiment knew no bounds. To the sick he afforded at his own expence, every comfort and nourishment, nor did those in health but experience his liberal bounties. He carried on a large trade in the Cornelian branch, large quantities of this valuable stone being found in the Country. He also carried on other business of Merchandize in a very large way and was immensely rich. His Stores in Town occupied nearly a third part of the City, and had a most beautiful Country seat near our Barracks which was allways open for the reception of the Officers.

It was still not unusual in this period for Englishmen to adopt Indian ways and dress, but of course it became frowned upon in the next decades, following the arrival of Christian evangelicals and the stricter social code of the Victorians.

We were here well supplied with Beef, the best I ever saw in the East. The Cattle in general very large, and of great strength. They are well adapted for Draught purposes. Good Wheat grows plentifully in most of this Province and abundance of Vegetables, particularly Sweet Potatoes and Carrots, Spirituous Liquors are scarce and what they have (called Dorroo) is supposed to be pernicious, altho I have drank much of it without experiencing any Ill effect from it.

But the greatest evil attending the Country, is its being infested with noted and daring thieves, who Robin Hood like (as we are fabulously informed) commit their villainies in Gangs, each Gang having its Chief. The only method used by travellers with any property, expecting to reach his destination in safety is to engage before he leaves the coast, one of those Free booters at a pretty good expence to protect him, many of whom are left on the road by the Commander for this purpose, they will bring you in safety, even should you pass thro the robbers Camp, so we may see there is honesty among Thieves.

The bold and public manner of their Commiting those acts leaves me to suppose they are licenced robbers, or that they at least deliver a share of their booties to the Rajah of the Province after making any Captures.

The Drum Major of the 75th named Sutherland, having been left behind the Regiment sick and being recovered and proceeding to join us was robbed of his all, even to the very skin, nearly in which state he joined us, and this not being the first time he was so served, made an oath that he would shoot the first man he met (Native) and was as good as his word, but as this happened to be one of the Army followers, the Drum Major was in much danger of losing his own life for the Act. However Colonel Clarke being just on the eve of leaving the Army, his successor at the repeated solicitations of the Officers of the Regiment was induced to grant him his enlargement.

Those depredations are not intirly confined to the Gangs but committed Individually, at night they would frequently crawl into the lines unseen by the Sentries and steal the Knapsack from under the soldiers head, which we generally in Camp use as a Pillow, and seldom a night passed but some one or other was robbed, even the Rings from womens fingers have been by these light fingered Gentry taken off whilst sleeping, when at the same time each Tent had a man in turn nightly to detect them, but without effect.

Perhaps the reader may wish to enquire what became of Captain Williamson, whom I formerly mentioned as being dispatched by the Commanding Officer with a message to the Rajah of Kurria and detained by him.

I should before have told him that on taking possession of the Garrison he again joined us in good health, as did also many others whom the fate of War had left in the Rajahs power. They had all been well treated and gave much praise to the Enemy for humanity, a blessing seldom experienced by any thus unhapily placed. Perhaps the Rajah might be induced to act thus lenient, expecting should he fail in the defence of his Garrison to receive better terms, and in which I doubt not, he was not disapointed.

Parker his principle General also surrendered to us, and was treated in every respect as a Gentlemen. I saw him often after, but never knew in what capacity he was employed. I dare say he brought off a good purse and was perhaps glad of this opportunity of so doing it, being probably the only one that would ever have offered to him.

After a stay of about four months, we left Cambay and proceeded on a route towards Brodera, distant about 30 miles, on our arrival were Encamped at about a Mile distant from the Fort, which was at the time in possession of Arabs, but on whose account they maintained it I know not, and after remaining here about six weeks, we were ordered to Besiege it. Previous to which, however, those Runagates had committed many robberies on us, and had murdered a Corporal of our Regiment, but for whose death we hanged the Assasins without trial or order from anyone, their dying words were that they were only sorry at not being able to kill the whole of us, but seemed satisfied that their Comrades would complete what they had begun, but in this they were mistaken.

The Troops employed on this occasion was the 75th and 86th Regiments, one Regiment of British and two of Native Company Troops. The Siege was long and tiresome, and am sorry to say Indifferently conducted.

Colonel Woodington of the Companys Service had the Command, but owing to a dislike the Officers in general had to him, particularly those of the 75th, everything went awkward and his orders reluctantly complied with. We got possession of the Town which is close under the Garrison walls with great ease and lost only a man or two in the attempt, but afterwards in destroying some old houses to make room for a breaching Battery, a liquor storehouse was discovered, to which the men for a considerable time had free access without the knowledge of the Officers who were astonished at their ungovernable conduct. At first they could not believe it proceeded from Drunkeness, thinking it impossible to procure liquor for the purpose, but the mistery was at last unravelled, and the spirits destroyed. After this, matters went on more smooth for a few days when the Enemy thought proper to leave the Garrison to ourselves, taking however, everything valuable and moveable with them.

The 86th Regt under Captain Temple, in dislodging a body of them from a position they had taken near a Tank outside the Ramparts, gained much praise from the Commander, and if their behaviour on that occasion merited praise, I think it was the only circumstance during the Siege that did deserve any, and I am sure it was the only given.

Our Regiment was now in a very sickly state. Major Gray, our Commanding Officer had died, much to our sorrow, he was a most excellent Gentleman. Lieut MColl soon followed, and Lieutenants Weston and Harvey killed. They were all buried in one grave and near them a great many non-Commissioned Officers and Privates, some killed and others died of Fever complaints, Fluxes etc. A small neat monument with an Apposite Inscription was erected to their Memory at the Expense of the Regiment.

One man of our Regiment was killed during the Siege by a chance shot from the Garrison, whilst his comrade was shaving him, the Ball passing under the Barbers Arm entered his mouth and Instantly killed him.

We in a few days after received orders to go in pursuit of Old Red Boots; for so we had named their Chief in concequence of their allways appearing in that uniform, but they being principally Cavalry had proceeded many days march from us, and had united their forces with those of another Upstart named

Canoogee. Their joint forces were now Treble our number. And after some days we came up with them unawares encamped behind a thick wood having a large river in front of them, those are the situations they generally if possible make sure of for that purpose having great numbers of Cattle allways accompanying them.

> *"Old Red Boots" was the Gaekwar of Baroda, one of the principal Mahratta chiefs. The regimental history also mentions "Conojie", described as a refractory chieftain. This action took place in February 1803.*

The greater part of the Enemys forces were on our arrival, at the river fishing as we were afterwards informed, but with all these advantages, we made an ugly job of it.

To enter his Camp we had a long and very narrow defile to pass through which we were passing with our Field train of Artillery, but which in a short time became perfectly jamnd up and the passage rendered Totally impassable, this gave time to the Enemy to collect his forces and we were soon surrounded. Fireing upon us from the Banks above and from the Tops of Trees killed a great number of men. What became of our Officers, we knew not, two or three only remaining with us, and thus situated we soon followed them.

Lieut Colonel Holmes the Commander of the party now put himself at the head of it and in a bold and gallant stile, carried all before him with the Bayonet, and had this Officer done so at the first, a number of brave men had been saved. It was not indeed his duty to have done so, now being the Chief in Command, and many will Ignorently say what is the use of an Officer In Action. This I know and that I believe the most Ignorant are now convinced off from the many and recent successes of the Great Wellington, and the failures of Others, that a brave and experienced Officer is half, and I may add the whole of the Battle, provided he be well supported by the inferior Officers and

Soldiers, which must of course follow.

The Ill success which had now for a time attended us reminds me of the failures of the Israelites after turning from God and bowing to Idols. We certainly had sufficiently transgressed to deserve his Anger and doubted not but our misfortunes were in great measure heaped upon us through our evil deeds, but I am running wide from my narrative and should I continue you will say, I have dropt the Idea of concluding my history and am attempting to write a Sermon.

After having driven the Enemy to the opposite banks of the River we buried our dead and removed our shattered remains back to Camp, the Commander not thinking it advisable to follow them any longer, we there remained a few weeks and commenced another route, which ended in several severe marches to no purpose, when towards the close of the fair season, the 75th received Orders to march to Surat and Winter. Our very weak, and sickly (not to say ragged) state much requireing it, here we arrived and took up Barracks in the City, but this in a short time was found not to have the desired effect of recovering our sick, on the Contrary they dayly increased and many Died. We in concequence removed to a plain where Cantoonments had been erected for our reception, and shortly after our men began rapidly to recover.

> *The Governor of Bombay, in recognition of its 'distinguished gallantry, and high and meritorious service' over the past year, awarded the Regiment a month's extra field allowance, although they were by then back in barracks. In view of WK's comments on pay and allowances, it is to be wondered if the troops saw much of this.*

This is a large City formerly subject to the Mogul, whose Flag is still flying on a seperate staff with that of the British. The revenues however are received by the Company who carry on a large trade here. The City or Citys (being two, the one surrounding the other, and well defended by a Castle) is but an Ill looking place. Narrow Streets clouded with dust, and the great heat of the Climate renders it a very disagreable and unhealthy retreat for which reason few only but those in a Mercantile way seldom reside here. The houses are flat roofed to which the Inhabitants repair in the Evenings to enjoy the Air and offer their devotions. The women are remarkably cleanly and industrous.

Here is an Hospital Established and Maintained at the expense of the Natives for Sick and infirm Animals. Horses, Oxen, Asses, Dogs etc enjoy the benefit of this Institution, when at the same time numbers of their fellow creatures are lying in the open streets expiring and starving without a look of pity.

This is the station appointed for the residence of the Companys Admiral, who is chosen from the Senior Naval Captains, his Command exists for three years when his successor is appointed and the Old one retires, no doubt well loaded, they have no Authority whatsoever over His Majestys Navy.

An English Gentleman residing here of the name of N. Crowe Esq Officiating in the Capacity of Judge and Magistrate found Abundance of employ by means of our Regts arrival in reforming the Abuses and dishonest practices of it.

From the date of the Regiments arrival in India to the period of our arrival in this Garrison, nearly Seventeen Years had elapsed and no Settlement made, I mean not to say the Balances were not struck, this was done every two months regularly, and signed, but Cash not issued except a trifling dayly issue exclusive of our provisions and necessary clothing, the Ballances therefore accumulating from Arrears was detained by the Captains in charge of Companys. And at the decease of Individuals the Funeral Expences, that is the amount of a coffin if circumstances admitted it, was paid by that Gentleman, the remainder was the Officers, no matter whether the deceased left any Will, a Brother near relation Or any consanquinity whatever (Wife excepted). This became the property of the Officer, and to Offer to demand it, or indeed your Own arrears was a Crime Capital, and as such severely punished. It appeared by the manner of their twisting the meaning of the Articles of War on this head about, that the whole were compiled for this one Henious Offence, they being generally convicted on different sections of this learned Code and examplary punished.

But this at last was put a stop to by the exertions of the Judge, to whom they were dayly applying by Dozens (commonly headed by the Sergeant Major the most active in the business) with Wills if they had any such documents, if not their Affadavits was taken and deemed sufficient, the Copy of which countersigned by the Judge with a request of Payment was then sent by him to the Commanding Officer. But the greatest Obsticle now was to find the money as many of the Officers had Died or left the Regiment as it materially assisted them in purchasing Promotion and those who still remained were without the Will or what was worse the means of answering the demand. This however they were at last by some means or other obliged to do not only by the Orders of the Magistrate, but also the Commanding Officer Lieut Colonel Watson who had just joined the Regiment from England and seemed happy at the opportunity offering of enforceing the Judges Orders previous to his taking on himself the Command.

This being as far as practicable complied with, we ever after received our just demands monthly, nor had we any trouble after in recovering what might be due to a Deceased Comrade, provided Witnesses were present to attest hearing the Testator say he left all he had to such a particular person, and this I make no doubt was often done without any such circumstance taking place, and the money divided between the Witnesses and supposed Legatee.

> *Pay and allowances were still very largely in the hands of the regimental officers. A sum was allocated to pay for a certain number of men and the officers were free to do very much what they liked with it, and abuses like the one described*

were still common.

The Common drink used here, as also that in most parts of India is extracted from the Sprouts of the Cocoanut Tree and called Toddy. When fresh drawn It is of a pleasant sweet taste, somewhat resembling Cyder, but if kept for any length of time becomes Tart and soon sour if exposed to heat. It is also of an Intoxicating nature, and by distillation produces a strong spirit called Dorroo which to an European at first drinking appear Nauseous, but this we were frequently obliged to be content with after failure of Arrack, the best sort of which we were formerly supplied with from Batavia. Latterly however, this could not be obtained, as the Dutch and English were not on good terms and Batavia being in possession of the former, but in some degree to remedy this, they had recourse to distilling of Rum, and which at this time I dare say is equal to that of Jamaica, but particularly that distilled at Salsette in Bombay, and that of Patna in Bengal.

The Cocoanut Tree is certainly the most useful tree in the world. The tree however of itself, that is the trunk of it, is but of little value except for firewood, and its produce of Toddy, which brings a ready sale and good profit. But the shell of the nut if properly managed, may be made into many valuable Articles particularly drinking Cups etc.

The Husk of the Shell after being striped is manufactured into Ropes of all descriptions, from a Ships Cable to a Horse Halter, and from that to all sorts of small Cordage which is very useful.

The Kernel of the Nut is agreable and wholesome eating when necessitated to use it for that purpose, but more particularly useful in Cooking if not too long gathered, but if it should become putred and desolves itself into a sort of Jelly, it is then pressed and produces excellent oil which is used for many purposes, such as in Cookery, Surgery, and Colours etc. It also contains a considerable quantity of what is called Milk within the shell which is both pleasant and harmless drinking. The Branches when plaited together is used for covering the Houses or Huts of the lower sort of people which answers very well in preventing the entrance of rain, and will continue for a long time provided it be not destroyed by the White Ant or other insects to which it is very liable.

The Toddy is also used by Bakers to leaven the bread with, without which as there are no Brewerys in this part it would be a difficult matter to provide a substitute to answer this purpose.

This Liquor is drawn from the Young Sprouts twice each day. An earthern pot being suspended to each sprout receives the droping liquid and the greatest trouble seemingly to a spectator is the ascending and descending the tree for it, but as the Natives are very dexterous in the Art of Climbing this is thought nothing of. A poor man having Twenty or Thirty of those Trees surrounding his little dirty Hut enjoys that peace and Tranquility of life which those in a palace may be strangers to.

Chapter 6

A New Enemy
1804 - 1806

I shall now take my leave of this quarter of India and proceed with my reader towards Bengal, having received orders for Embarkation and vessels being arrived to transport us we with raptures obeyed the order and in a few days found ourselves again in Bombay Harbour, where we remained about a fortnight, but did not disembark. Here Detachments of the 61st and 88th Regts (left behind their Corps on their proceeding to Egypt) joined us, being turned over to the 76th Regiment as drafts. The whole occupying four ships. We had a very unpleasant passage from Bombay, and our vessel (the Jane) in particular was in great danger of being lost, being very ill mand. with Country Sailors, who owing to the rough treatment received from their Officers seemed rather to prefer death to life.

In the Bay of Bengal the vessel was caught in a squall under full sail, which the sailors could or would not strike until the Ship was laying on her beam ends. The Chief Officer was himself an Excellent sailor but a cruel Tyrant, and happily the squall (as is common in those seas) was but for a short duration. We somehow got her again righted, and safely arrived in the Hoogly river which in a few hours by the assistance of an able Pilot and a good tide brought us opposite the beautiful and strong Garrison of Fort William where we dropt Anchor and the next day landed.

The Regiment arrived in Calcutta in May 1804 to join the

army under Lord Lake in a campaign against the Mahratta chief Holkar in the Upper Provinces.

The most beautiful views that ever met the eye presents itself in sailing down this fine River. The current carries a vessel very rapidly down and the many Elegant seats, Gardens etc on its Banks presents itself in an instant, as if rising by the Art of Magic and again as suddenly disappearing, is among the many delightful Objects offering itself to the Amazed Spectator. Mango Groves, Shady Walks, Sportive Animals, and the conceited Peacock are delightfull sights to the half shipwrecked sailor returning to enjoy the pleasures of the India Capital which a few hours before he had but distant hopes of ever viewing, all cares or thoughts of death then vanish as instantaniously as the rough billows disappear and Portsmouth or Plymouth like the Bottle and Lass ingrosses his whole attention, but it is fifty to one on his return to Ship that he has soon occasion to repent of his connection by being not only eased of his money but for many months labouring under a disorder severe enough in a frigid but much worse in a torrid climate, and which frequently ends but with Death in either.

After remaining here some weeks, vessels were provided to carry us to the Upper Provinces. Our destination at first being Cawnpore, the distance by water is said to be 1100 miles owing to the Serpentine course of the rivers, but I should suppose that by land it may be reduced to one half or probably two thirds of that number of miles. The estimated time and Pay in Advance for this trip generally being four months, two of which are issued on leaving the Presidency and the other two at Benares, being about half the way.

To Equip a Regiment for this change of Quarters is certainly attended with great expence, every attention being paid to the comforts of those concerned, and as the conveyance is on small undecked vessels covered over with Thatch or a suitable substitute, which answers the double purpose of preventing the soldiers from the exposure of both rain and heat. Probably twenty men or women, children etc. may be accomodated in each boat, more or less according to the boats dimensions, sometimes proceeding under sail but more frequently under tow by the boatmen who land for that purpose. At night the whole are drawn up in line close in shore to which you may descend from the vessel by a plank being thrown over. Little duty on this command is required from the soldiers and I can with confidence say that this together with my subsequent return by the same method of conveyance were the most delightful of my days spent in His Majestys Service.

Many Magnificent Mosques and Temples, Citys and Palaces, together with beautiful Military Stations are to be passed previous to arrival at Cawnpore, the most principle of which are Berhampore, Dinapore, Gazapore, Monghier, Benares, Patna and Allahabad. The English soldiers in time of Peace generally occupy Berhampore, Dinapore and Allahabad, the others are most frequently Garrisoned by Seapoys with a proportion of British Artillery. I mean those of the Companys Service. Silk Spinning and Weaving, Indigo Manufactorys etc employs numbers of hands of both sexes from the Child to the great Grandparents. Salt Petre, Cotton and many other Commoditys are abundant, as also Grain and Cattle, which latter are by the Natives made but little use of except for Milk. Their religion, I before observed, prohibiting them eating Animal Food.

The rivers, especially the Ganges, are greatly Infested with Allegators and large Snakes, but from the Partiality of the Natives to bathing together with its forming a part of their religious Worship, they are nevertheless commonly three or four times a day in the water altho as I have been informed are often devoured by those dread monsters in the attempt. This is considered a happy omen for the future state and doubtless sometimes Voluntaryly suffered.

Persons near death are brought to the side of the river on their Beds and sometimes before the soul is disengaged the body and accompanyments are tumbled into the water by their unconcerned relatives who seem to rejoice at the event. Many dead bodies are to be seen floating with the current on this voyage. A most unpleasant and nausious sight to those of a Fastidious Stomach to which nearly everyone in part are subject in Sultry Climates. The Allegator will not devour dead carcases but rarely, otherwise the living would have more favourable chances of escapeing.

At Allahabad the Ganges and Nerbudda rivers cross each other, which causes a senceable motion to the Passengers, somewhat similar to the movements on ship board in the Bay of Biscay in calm weather, which causes sickness to those who have never before experienced it, and should the weather be rough, as it very frequently happens, the boats are in much danger of being lost, and many men have here perished.

WK means the River Jumna, which joins the Ganges here. The Nerbudda flows from the Deccan into the Arabian Sea near Baroda.

This Garrison has within those few years been totally rebuilt and was not finished when I last past there in the year 1805. It has a Magnificent Citidel said to have been founded by Acbar.

Monghier is a small Ill defended Garrison, the walls very weak and nearly destitute of Artillery. Invalids do its duty which is nominal. The river furnishes them with dainty fish if they are not to Independant to catch them and their Native Wives provide them every other necessary comfort in abundance.

Benares is a regular well built Town and the adjacent cantonments are delightful, far passing any place I ever saw in either Europe or Africa.

About Eight years since a most bloody Massacre was committed here on the English residents by a Vizier (called the Vizier Ally) but he was shortly afterwards apprehended through means of a brother on conditions that his life should be spared.

This was religiously adhered to but the Vizier was conducted in chains to Calcutta where he has since remained in an Iron Cage about Ten feet square without any attendance of the Natives except a cook, nor are any allowed to visit him, his Guards excepted, which as far as practicable is performed by Europeans, he is a very well looking man and speaks good English.

      Patna on the banks of the Ganges has very high walls but slender, the buildings also are of great height. Its streets narrow and dusty and the Inhabitants ferocious and unfriendly. This is a good trading City, distant from Calcutta about Four Hundred and Fifty Miles.

      On arrival at Cawnpore we disembarked having been about three months on boats, and went into Barracks vacated by the 76th Regiment. These Barracks are built on a desert plain near the river. There are however, some handsome Gardens attached to the Officers Houses but which are better adapted for shew than benefit their produce being immaterial, their defeciency is nevertheless amply supplied in the Bazar (or Market) where Vegetables etc are well supplied on moderate terms, persons being provided to regulate it and see It furnished from the neighbouring more fruitful country.

      The force of the sun is so powerful here in the sultry months, that numbers are struck instantly dead with it, nor is it possible at times to go bare footed out of Barracks, the heat being so great that brute Animals such as Dogs etc cannot set their feet on the ground. The Barrack walls formed of Mats, as also the Canvas Tents are constantly kept wet by throwing water on them by persons employed for the purpose, which gives them a more temperate degree.

      At this time the Grand Army (as it was called) under the late Lord Lake was before the Garrison of Dieg and it was thought not advisable to employ the 75th on that Siege probably to enable the besiegers to obtain the greater Prize, we therefore remained here some weeks before our order arrived to join them afterwards (in order to be at hand should necessity require it) and were marched to Muttra within twelve or fourteen miles of the Army where we remained till the Capture a few days after and then joined them on their route towards Bhurtpore.

      The Troops forming this Army previous to our arrival consisted of the 76th Regt, two Flank Companys of the 22nd Regt, Bengal European Regiment, some Companys of Artillery and about twelve Battalions of Native Infantry. The 8th, 25th and 27th Lt. Dragoons, and some Battalions of Native Dragoons with this force His Lordship had made many captures. The Great Mogul had been by his subjects deposed and his eyes put out. He was again restored to his Kingdom after the Capture of his Capital from the Insurgents and the ring leaders of the cruel conspiracy of Delhi punished with death. Agra also his second Capital was restored to him. Laswarree, Dieg and many other inferior Garrisons fell into His Lordships hands during this and the preceeding year, and he hoped to end his brilliant campaigns with the fall of Bhurtpore, but in this attempt the Army in three successive attacks were completely foiled.

*   The fortress of Bhurtpore was vast, with a circumference of at least eight miles, having a huge mud wall between eighty and a hundred feet high with a deep moat. The fact was that General Lake really had too few troops, guns or engineers for the task, which was made more difficult by the presence of large numbers of Holkar's cavalry in the vicinity. Lake's cavalry were fully occupied in keeping these at a distance, so the job of protecting the British camp fell more heavily on the infantry, who had also to provide escorts for foraging parties and convoys. Lake's impatience and lack of planning contrast badly with Wellesley's successful campaign further south culminating in his triumph at Assaye.*

*   The 76th had fought several major battles earlier in the campaign, and were very experienced in sieges.*

      The first attempt we made on this remarkable strong fortress was about the middle of November. The storming party was under the command of Lieut Colonel Maitland of the 75th who had a few weeks before joined the Regt. This attack seemed at first to offer fair for success, but all favourable appearances soon vanished, for on the partys arrival near the Walls found it surrounded by a wet ditch and at most parts unfordable, this occasioned much time and after about the one third or probably more had got footing on the opposite side, and were attempting to posses the breach, the Enemy who had all this time been viewing us now commenced a more destructive fire from his masked Batterys and Ramparts with upwards of Two Hundred Pieces of Cannon which soon thined our Ranks and killed the Commander with most of the other Officers. The remainder thus circumstanced and deeming any further attempts for the night folly, the survivors were marched back to camp. The loss on this attempt was great and His Lordship found himself under the necessity of sending to Bombay for reinforcements, the Army of that Presidency being still employed in Guzerat.

   Previous to their Arrival all preparations were made for a second attack. Boats made of basket work and covered with the skins of Goats or other Animals and scaling ladders were prepared, but through an error of the Engineer neither answered; the Ladders were much too short.

> On 13th February the colonel issued an a regimental order that, although the men of the 75th had declined any additional payment for digging trenches, as other troops were receiving it, it should still be paid to the regiment.

   During this interval the Rajah was on the Alert preparing for defence as was the besiegers for Offence, and the Bombay Army under General Jones being arrived a second attack was made but with no better success.

   This second attempt failing after arrival of so large assistance much damped the spirit of all the more, so having heretofore been

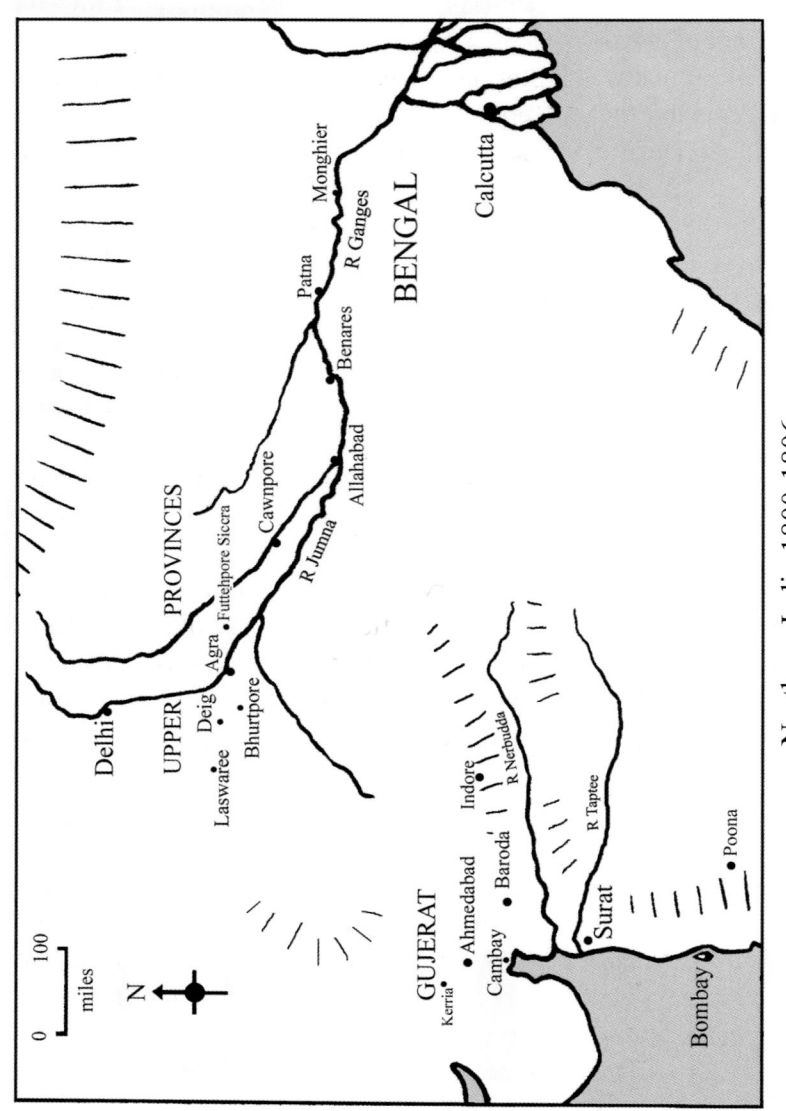

Northern India 1800-1806

generally conquerors.

The Troops brought from Bombay by General Jones were the 65th 86th and Bombay European Regiment with six Battalions of Seapoys.

This attack was under the Commd of Lieut Colonel MacRae of the 76th and the loss equally severe as the former.

A Third Attempt was soon in forwarding, and nearly all hands imployed on it. This was conducted by the Honble. Colonel Monson of the 76th. When after many desperate efforts to carry the breach as also to escalade the walls without effect and the party being greatly diminished the brave Colonel was under the necessity of bringing off the survivors as far as practicable, but from the number of Wounded, many were left in the Rajahs Power and carried prisoners into the fort where they were well treated.

Thus ended our three Ill fated attempts on Bhurtpore, and with it the War. For altho we had in the whole been unfortunate, yet the Rajah was fully convinced our failure was not attributable to want of either skill or bravery but to unsurmontable obsticles and expecting it was the determination of Lord Lake at all risks to get possession of the Garrison, he came to the resolve of sueing for terms. What they were I know not, but whatever they might be were immediately accepted and we shortly after left Bhurtpore and with the wish of all I believe concerned never again to visit it.

There were in fact four attempts, and the preparations for yet another, together with Lake's success in driving away and defeating Holkar's Mahratta cavalry, persuaded the Rajah to sue for terms on the 10th March. WK's description of the siege of Bhurtpore, which cost the lives of over three thousand British troops, is an essentially accurate and useful addition to the more detailed accounts elsewhere, but is one of the very few ranker's eyewitness accounts.

The day after the Articles were agreed on, the Rajah paid a visit in person to the Commander in Chief, which was likely to be attended with Ill concequences. He was a good looking person mounted on an Elephant, seated under a rich canopy (or as it is often called, a castle) having on the left of him one of his sons, and guarded by about four hundred of his men, Cavalry and Infantry, the latter were all dressed in the stript clothing of our slain. The Europeans you may be sure were exasperated at their audacity, but the Seapoys became furious and in a few minutes neither Rajah or attendants would have been in existence but for the timely interposition of His Lordship who exhorted the seapoys to depart peaceably, which they did, but we never after saw any of his men in our Camp in the British uniform. It is not an uncommon thing in a Seapoy Battalion to see several whole familys accompany it. A son having enlisted soon persuades his brother to do the same, that brother another and so on. The sisters they contrive to get married to a favorite Comrade. The Father and Mother finding themselves thus deprived of their children frequently accompany them and are subsisted at their expence.

No doubt these men were the more exasperated at the Rajah and his escort in concequence of the deaths of their Brothers or near relations who might have fallen by them, and appearing before them in the very clothing which a day or two before were worn in their ranks, this appeared to them (and I think very natural although probably unintentional on the part of the Enemy) a great insult.

I should have before mentioned the brave spirit of the few remains of the 22nd Flank Companys. They left Calcutta under Captain Lindsey for the purpose of joining the Army in the field and consisted at first of Two Hundred and Ten Rank and File with their complement of Officers and Serjeants; on the last attack on Bhurtpore the whole remaining of them consisted of one Sergeant and Eighteen Rank and File, they were in concequence ordered to remain in Camp. Yet contrary to orders given them they put themselves in motion and accompanied the Party where they left six of the remaining small number dead, and the Serjeant whose name was Shipp was wounded. He was afterwards promoted to Ensign and from that to Lieutenant in the 76th Regiment, but having a desire to return again to India disposed of his Commission at Jersey and Enlisted as a private in the 8th Light Dragoons and if living is now with them in Bengal.

John Shipp published his remarkable story in 1829 (after WK's death) and it remained popular reading throughout the nineteenth century. Actually it was the 24th Dragoons in which Shipp re-enlisted, worked his way up to Sergeant-Major, and was then appointed Ensign in the 87th Regt.

It would have been impossible had not terms been agreed on to have done but little more this Campaign. The rains having partially commenced and the weak and crippled state of the Army afforded no hopes of conquest, had the attempt been made nothing more could have been afforded from the Artillery or Engineer Department. It would therefore have been rashness and extreme folly, and the whole Army might have considered itself as engaging on a Forlorn Hope. Another attempt would doubtless have failed and left us in a state unable to defend ourselves from an Enemys Attack, which would certainly have followed, but this did not happen and the Army was shortly after distributed into Winter Quarters.

The Bombay Army proceeding back a march of many hundred miles to its Presidency. The European Infantry of the Bengal Army consisting of the 75th, 76th and Bengal Regiment occupied Futtypore Siccra, an Old Garrison about forty miles from Agra and one hundred and fifty from Cawnpore.

Here the 76th Received orders to proceed to England on ships of the season, such men as chose to remain in the Country were allowed a bounty which most of them received to join the 75th Regiment.

The 76th joining the 75th persuaded me that the 75th would

never return to England, which after an absence of Eighteen Years I was foolishly inclined to do, and having communicated my desires to my good friends Captain Engel Acting Paymaster and Lt Mathewson Adjutant they obtained for me leave to effect an Exchange which I soon did by giving Fifty rupees to my successor.

    I have frequently considered with myself since exchanging whether or not I could have been perfectly sane at the time. I may call it by what name I chose, but the gentlest appellation I could possibly put on it could not be less than folly. To leave a Corps to which I was well known and respected and from which I received many good benefits to purchase an exchange into a Regiment to whom I was a perfect stranger when at the same time I had not a distant hope (nor I may add a wish) to leave the Service, also the subsequent return of my old Corps on the following Year, from whom I was certain exertions had been made and would be continued to my Interest to give it the easiest term possible must be said to have been Folly and ungratitude, particularly so to my best of Friends, Captn Engel to whom I was Clerk or more properly speaking Paymaster Serjeant of the Regiment as also Pay Serjeant of two Companies and Nominal Armourer Serjeant for the time from all of which Situations I received the emoluments and pay allowed for them by the East India Company.

*   The company pay sergeant was a sought-after post, and would have involved reponsibility for equipment and clothing as well as pay. This equates to a modern company quartermaster sergeant, a warrant officer class two appointment, as would be the regimental orderly room sergeant, or as WK describes it, the Clerk to the Adjutant. It would appear that WK was the second most senior NCO in the Regiment after the Sergeant Major.*

    The Captain as I before observed having endeavoured thus

far to indulge me had however after attainment of my object been sorry for it and used his endeavours to urge me to drop the Idea of Exchanging to remain with him another Year, when he assured me he expected the 75th would follow, if not something better should be provided for me, but I thought matters had been carried too far to recant as both parties had joined their Regiments agreable to exchange and neither seemed willing to depart from his former resolution.

    I had also another motive which was a bar to it, should I have been more strongly inclined. A Comrade Sergeant named Robert Emslie had also exchanged and we both promised not to part. It would therefore have been a great breach of solemn promise in either to have thought afterwards of remaining, particularly so in me as I found him totally adverse to staying longer in India, we therefore stuck to our promises and accompanied each other home and were afterwards fellow sufferers on some very unfortunate Services for our pains.

>   *To be fair to WK, the 76th had fought alongside the 75th in the desperate actions at Bhurtpore, and no doubt he had many friends in the other Regiment. Due to the extensive cross-postings over the years while the regiments had been in India, the make up of both was likely to have been similar, and the proportion of Scots remaining in the 75th relatively low. In fact 300 men from the 76th were transferred to the 75th at this time. In 1809, the Horse Guards decided that several "Highland" Regiments, the 75th among them, contained so few Highlanders that they should cease to be called Highland, and no longer wear Highland dress.*
>
>   *Despite the assumptions of many nineteenth century painters back in England, no Highland regiments actually wore the kilt in India at this time.*

    All arrangements being made for the 76th Regiments departure, about three weeks after commencement of its drafting we proceeded to Cawnpore, having only the Officers, compliment of Non Commissioned Officers, Drummers and Invalids to escort the Colours home. At Cawnpore we took boats and proceeded in a similar manner I before related, nothing worthy of notice occured during the passage except the passing of Sir Geo Barlow, Deputy Governor and his retinue proceeding to the Upper Provinces. Earl Cornwallis the Governor General having also attempted to do the same but died after performing about half of his Journey and his remains Deposited in a vault at Gauzapore but from whence I have been informed they have been removed to England. He died much regretted by all, but none more than the Native Princes and Chiefs. His Lordship having some years before held this High and Important situation, they were no strangers to his wisdom and virtue, nor were they Ignorant of his strict and impartial manner of administering Justice to all men of whatever rank in Life.

Cornwallis had been reappointed at the age of 67 as Governor-General to succeed Wellesley, who had fallen out of favour with the Government in London. He died on 5th October 1805 at Ghazipore after only two months in office, being succeeded by his deputy Sir George Barlow. Cornwallis had reversed Wellesley's policy and made peace with the Mahrattas, greatly to their advantage, so they had good reason to regret his death.

We arrived at Calcutta about the latter end of this Year, and the ships on which we were to embark not having arrived, we remained in Garrison till the following February.

Having no men to perform the Garrison duty this was an Idle period for us, and having little else to engage my attention I of a sudden became Mistically inclined and speedily got Initiated into the secrets of Free Masonry. Having made some progress in the several degrees I continued and finished them in England and

Ireland at leasure opportunities.

The Indiamen having arrived we Embarked on four ships, viz. Lady Castlereagh, Surry, Lord Duncan and Walpole. I was with Head Quarters the Castlereagh.

As those ships were all very heavy laden, little room was left to accomodate the few of us, but sufficient enough for a warm climate, as we seldom remained long below decks. We sailed in a few days after Embarkation for the Island of Ceylon, being the Rendezvous appointed for Homeward bound ships from China, Bengal, Bombay and Madras. We left Point De Gall about the middle of March and was favoured with a pretty good voyage without touching anywhere but the Island of St Helena on our return. This Island being now the alloted residence of the fallen French Emperor, many accounts have been given of it more perfectly than I am able, and as I never was in the interior of it can have no idea of anything but the landing place which brings you in an Instant into the Village.

It is interesting that WK does not mention either the action involving a large French frigate "Le Cannonier" and the escort HMS Tremendous on 21st April or the storm on the 24th, both of which are noted in the Regimental history. Both warships were badly damaged but the Frenchman was driven off. These incidents occurred off the coasts of Madagascar and Natal. An Indiaman, The Prince of Wales, had been lost in a storm in these waters only two years before.

John Shipp, who was in the Indiaman Lord Duncan, described the storm as follows: "...we were overtaken by a terrific hurricane, which blew for two days without a pause. During the course of it the Lady Castlereagh seemed certain to be lost. She was about a quarter of a mile from us, and we watched her as she heeled over so violently that at one time we could see the whole of her keel. There was a shout of horror from all of us at the sight of it, and our Captain said she would never right herself. But the next wave brought her up, and though she rolled, and pitched, and laboured dreadfully she kept afloat. Some of her masts were carried away, but which I do not now recollect. She was the only vessel in the fleet to suffer much damage."

I call it a Village but it bears the name of I think James' Town, everything was then remarkably dear except Mackrell and Water Cresses but it must be now I should suppose much worse having not only several great personages of all nations, but a Treble Military Force.

When we called there the only troops doing duty were a few Companys Soldiers, Artillery and Infantry and a very rough set they seemed to be. Some of our men having been frolicsome enough inclined to sleep on shore were not only robbed of their money but Shoes, Stockings, Jackets etc were stript from them and they came from land in a similar state they came from their mothers womb, or the state Uniform of Old King Adam on his Coronation.

The Bum-boats as they are called in England brought off some small Potatoes and Green Apples to us for sale, the former at Eighteen Shillings per Bushel and the latter at one Shilling each.

They would also oblige you by taking your washing (if you chused to trust them) at a shilling per shirt and other Articles proportionally reasonable, and upon the whole if Hell is to be found on earth I think St Helena is or then was the spot to look for it.

There is a brief note dated 17 July 1806 among the letters, written aboard ship off the Scillies to catch the Falmouth packet, warning his brother of his imminent arrival in England.

Chapter 7

A Different War
1806 - 1809

The Regiment landed in England in the month of August a few miles below Dartford in Kent and marched into that Town where we remained until our destination was fixed at the War Office, which was afterwards at Nottingham. When on our arrival were joined by four Officers and upwards of 150 Non-Commissioned and privates, this Town having for many years been the Regiments Depot.

On arrival at Dartford WK wrote to his brother with all his news, including why he was now with a different regiment. The letter is actually dated 24 July 1806, so his memory of the month of arrival was slightly at fault.
Lt. John Shipp was still with the Regiment while they were at Nottingham, but, detached to Wakefield with a recruiting party, fell into debt and sold his commission (not in Jersey as mentioned by WK earlier). He soon tired of civilian life and enlisted again, and then went back to India with the 24th Dragoons, where he was last heard of by WK. Extraordinarily, he was again commissioned, saw yet more action, and lived to retire to England.

Recruiting Parties were soon dispatched to the Neighbouring Towns and Counties so that we very soon found ourselves to be getting somewhat Efficient and removed to Lincoln being the residence of the Monson Family to whom our Colonel was nearly related. He was soon after chosen Member of Parliament for the

City but did not live long to enjoy it. He was something past the Meriden of Life and from long and fatiguing service in India together with many wounds he seemed to the sorrow of all to be fast approaching to his Grave and did not survive many months.

He certainly of all men was the greatest Honour to his Profession, Brave, Generous, Human and Tender as a Parent to those under his Command, but more particularly so to the Non-Commissioned and private, without any pride, and if he had any fault it was that of being too good to some indifferent characters.

He has often been heard to say he would rather himself suffer flogging than see it inflicting. On which account when these unpleasent parades took place which was absolutely necessary for examples too frequently, he was generally absent.

He was of a Noble Family. Uncle to the then Lord Monson of Burton near Lincoln, where to the sorrow of every Individual not only of the Regiment but City, we buried him. It may not here be improper to note a circumstance to the Honour of this worthy and lamented Officer and was as I have been informed as follows.

The Serjeant Major of the Regiment had thro the Colonels intrest and his own bravery been promoted in India to an Ensigncy which not being agreeable to some of the Officers, he having some years before unfortunately been punished for Intoxication. He was as usual after his Promotion invited by the Commanding Officer to join the Officers Mess. The first night of his appearance many of the Officers had agreed on his arrival to leave the Mess room through derision of him but the Colonel having notice of their Intentions made it convenient that night to attend himself which he seldom did being generally receiving or returning a dinner with Superior Officers of the Army.

On this night however, he attended arm in arm with Ensign Montgomery whom he seated next himself and during the whole of the evening the Colonels discourse was directed to none but him, and the other Officers seeing Wm Montgomery thus Honoured were afterwards very eager to court his friendship and Company.

Montgomery is believed to be one of only two men surviving who had sailed to India with the 76th in 1788.

Colonel Monson was undoubtedly a very brave and popular officer, but his time in command of an independant brigade in India in 1804 had been less successful. Becoming isolated in the Deccan by ignoring orders, his force had to beat an ignominious retreat to Agra, pursued by Holkar's Mahrattas. This British defeat, which showed the British were not invincible, greatly encouraged the Mahrattas. It had far reaching results, one being the decision of the Rajah of Bhurtpore to side with Holkar. General Wellesley commented "You will have heard of Monson's reverses: I tremble for the political consequences of these events".

Lt.Col.Michael Symes commanded the Regiment after Col Monson. He was to die of exhaustion very soon after embarking after the evacuation of Corunna in January 1809.

There is a sequence of letters from Nottingham with news of his activities and movements which illustrate the fact that the army was the only disciplined force of men available to the government to enforce civil order at this time, and so regiments at home not only had to recruit and train but to act as police generally and ensure order during elections.

In Letter 11, it is interesting that WK hints at the possibility of further promotion, which could only have been a commission as an Adjutant or Quartermaster. These appointments were often granted to senior non-commissioned officers, but were of course very much dependant on the recommendation of the Colonel. He was in the fortunate position of being well thought of by two regimental colonels. The reference to 'friends of rank in my own country', meaning Sussex, is also noteworthy, as commissioned rank was a much sought after status. No wonder he was so bitter at being deprived of sergeant's pay while on the Isle of Wight in 1811.

After a stay of a few months we left Lincoln having sufficiently Recruited the Regiment to be able to take the Island duties. We marched towards Portsmouth about the middle of June and embarked for Jersey, which we made in a few days, and after Disembarking marched to Grenville Barracks, the Eastern extremity of the Island, where we remained the whole of the time we were on the Island. About the latter end of this year volunteering from Militia into the line commenced and we soon received about Five Hundred men from the East and West Middlesex, Derby, Nottingham and Lincoln Regiments, this was the means of removing us back to England preparatory to more arduous service on the Continent.

Several letters from Jersey describe life on the island and speculate as to the future service of the Regiment. There is also mention of his shares of prize money from India.

The Honorary Colours granted to the Regiment by the East India Company for service in India had been approved by the King, and presented at a parade in St Helier on 27 January 1808.

The Channel Islands were strongly garrisoned throughout the Napoleonic Wars, but were never seriously threatened with invasion, partly because, lacking good harbours for larger warships, they were not seen as a threat. Modern standards of information security and censorship were unheard of, and WK was giving nothing away by writing home with details of the strength of the garrison, as trade and communication links with the French mainland were maintained unofficially, to the advantage of both sides.

But having brought the reader to Jersey and he perhaps not unacquainted with the game called Leap Frog, may not be satisfied with my taking a Jump over Channel and back again without saying something about it. I shall therefore (as the Jersey and English people are similar to next door neighbours) be but

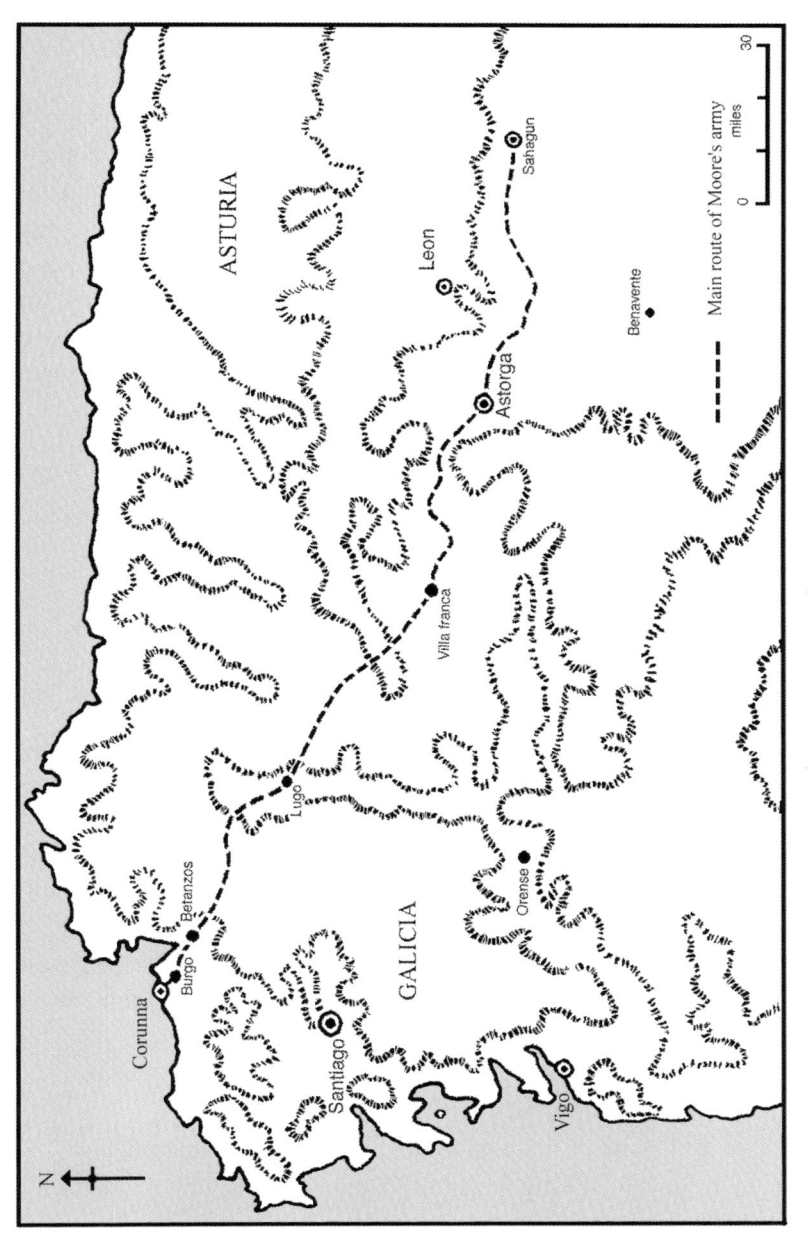

The Retreat to Corunna

brief in my description.

Jersey is a small Island in the English Channel near the coast of Normandy in France, to which Laws they are still subject. In circumference about Thirty Miles, containing, I believe, Twelve Parishes and the Capital is St Hilliers which is the residence of the Governor. It has a tolerable Harbour for vessels of light Tonnage but difficult of access being surrounded with rocks and shallows.

The people civil and sagacious and a trader must be thoroughly awake when dealing with them or he may depend on being cropooed. They are very slovenly in appearance, that is, the ordinary sort of them, but those somewhat more exalted in Life are much the reverse and generally very conceited and Proud.

It is a pleasent little spot and has various amusements as in England. They profess the Protestant Religion but from what I saw of them they pay but little attention to it

On our return to England we landed at Landguard Fort in Essex from whence we marched to Colchester Barracks. Here the Regiment underwent some smart discipline in consequence of drafts from many different Regiments of Militia whose exercise frequently differs much, but a stop was soon put to it by the Ophthalmia, a disorder in the Eyes, first I believe felt among the Troops employed in Egypt and returned with them from it, many of whom had been discharged totally blind thro it, and as this disease is contagious, many of our people caught it by sleeping on the same bedstead formerly used by them. We therefore removed to Danbury which was appointed the Opthalmia Depot, when from the excellent water and the best medical attendance the disorder soon disappeared and we marched to Ipswich Barracks where we remained till the month of August and marched to Harwich for Embarkation for Spain.

We sailed after Embarkation for Falmouth to join that part of the Expedition to arrive from Ireland under General Sir David Baird and remained in that Harbour some weeks awaiting their arrival and a short time after till the Commander had finished his arrangements and the wind soon becoming fair we sailed out of Harbour and arrived at Corunna about the middle of October where we were Brigaded and landed in succession. The Brigade to which we were appointed was under the command of Major General McKenzie consisting of the 59th, 60th and 76th Regiments which being, I believe the last Brigade landed caused us to remain some days on board after arrival as each Brigade after landing remained a day or perhaps two to prepare itself with the requisites for proceeding forward to join the Army under Sir Jn. Moore, concequently on the day of the first Brigade marching forward the second landed and occupied the Barracks the former vacated, and so on till the whole were put in motion.

The Barracks if so they may be called (but they do not deserve the name) are called St Lucie adjoining the Town, but as our stay in them was only for a night it would not be worth mentioning, was it not to the disgrace of that Beggarly Nation to say that short as the time was, it was sufficiently long to load us with Lice. But that matters nothing, for had we not got acquainted with those Vermin then we soon should elsewhere, as to all appearance from the Palace to the Cottage each has a share of those disgraceful and troublesome Insects.

Our Brigade moved forward about the 12th of Nov leaving the 60th regiment doing duty at Corunna the first day we arrived at Betanzes a smart little town enough. We then proceeded to Lugo three days march from hence this is a large City, having two convents for different orders of Friars of St Francesca and St Dominic - if any such saints may be found - in which we took up quarters and remained two or three days and marched to Saint Jago another larger City. Here also we were in Convents and remained some time, the Regiment being divided into many detachments of Escort. We afterwards received orders to march to Vigo, but the Orders were countermanded after our arrival at Compestella at which there is an University and many students of the Romish persuasion. We then marched back again to Saint Jago where we met the Advance of Sir Jn Moores Army in full retreat towards Corunna and afterwards accompanied them.

Saint Jago is about 120 miles distant from Corunna and the Army continued retreating until arrival there with occasionally halting an hour or two only, except at Lugo where it was intended to await the Arrival of the Enemy.

> *WK does not detail all the marching and countermarching the regiment carried out in November and December prior to the actual Retreat to Corunna. For example, on the 12th December, they marched from near Santiago to Lugo, a distance of 76 miles, in 48 hours. They were obviously already tired before the order to retreat was given by Sir John Moore on 23rd December.*
> *WK is mistaken about meeting Moore's army at Saint Jago. He must have meant Astorga.*

Here a smart action but of short duration took place in which our regiment had Six or Seven men killed or wounded and the Other Regts suffered more or less, after which we continued our retreat and the Enemy contented himself for the night in occupying the Town for refreshment but followed us next morning. Nothing afterwards occured till arrival at Corunna worthy of Notice.

> *This action mainly involved the Light Companies of the 76th and the 51st and 59th, with whom they were then Brigaded under Major General Leith.*

The Fatigues of this March, want of Nourishment and intense cold on the Mountains had nearly killed me, and several had died through its fatigues, and not a few frozen to death before our return to Betanzes, when I was totally unable to proceed farther. There Lieutenant and Adjutant Rooth (to whom I must ever remain a heavy debtor) mounted me on his Mule and sent a man to accompany, and keep me on his back to Corunna, where

I became in a state of Insensibility and so remained until after arrival in Plymouth Hospital about the latter end of January following.

Between Villa Franca and Lugo, a distance of 48 miles which was reached on 5th January, the Regiment lost over 45 men due to the extremely bad weather and bad country.

The Regimental history records that Lt and Adjutant B. Rooth, 'a deservedly popular officer', retired in 1826 after 20 years in the post, while the regiment was in Canada.

For WK, who was aged 41 and probably one of the older men in the Regiment, to have got so far was a considerable achievement. He was indeed fortunate, but was also regarded as a valuable man.

From what I have before related, the reader may conclude I can say but little more regarding Spain except that as I was afterwards Informed, Sir Jn. Moore was killed in the Action of the 16th and Sir D. Baird lost an Arm, the Command then devolved on Sir John Hope, who creditably brought off the Army.

The whole loss on the retreat together with those in Action was great, but not so heavy as might have been expected and many of those whom at first was supposed to have been killed or taken Prisoner, rejoined their Regiments afterwards in England, having been kept concealed and afterwards assisted by the Spanish people (generally Friars) and in this particular much praise is due to that nation.

Excluding officers, the Regiment had 784 men fit for duty on first arriving at Corunna, but only 614 disembarked in England afterwards. As it had not been much engaged in the defence of Corunna, nearly all these casualties were due to the extreme conditions of the retreat. However, as WK notes later, a number who had become separated from the Regiment were rescued by the local inhabitants, conducted safely to Portugal and, with other survivors, became part of locally formed detachments and eventually joined the main body of the Army in Portugal.

On 8th December 1808 Lt Col. Symes had been sent by Gen. Baird to Leon for a personal report on the state of the Spanish army under General Romana, and did not rejoin his regiment until just before the battle of Corunna five weeks later. His death from exhaustion immediately after embarking is therefore understandable. Although WK does not mention the Spanish, their lack of support and co-operation during the campaign, with the notable exception of the population of Corunna, was the major factor in its failure. Both Moore and Baird were continually exasperated and misled by empty Spanish promises.

The road from St Jago to Corunna is very favourable to a retreating Army as a great part of it is between two high and inaccessible mountains and several Bridges to pass, which if properly blown up would have delayed the Enemy from following us, but this Attempt allways failed and I shall say no more on the unpleasant Subject.

The engineers had been notably unsuccessful in properly destroying most of the bridges during the retreat, and when tasked with the blowing of the last one at Burgo, had used such an excess of powder that one of the rearguard was killed and several badly injured by flying masonry.

The landing of the Troops in England was not without much confusion in concequence of the rapid manner of embarking at Corunna the Regiments were unavoidably intermixed and it was many weeks before they could account for their own numbers after arrival. There was not I believe a seaport in all England but some of the different Corps were left in it. About Thirty of the 76th among which number was myself were disembarked at Plymouth and sent to differents Hospitals there and great attention paid to our recovery.

Our Colours were marched to Ipswich by a few of the Regiment and in course of time all those who survived joined them there.

I remained but a few weeks in a Hospital, there not being accommodation for the half requiring admittance. Therefor as soon as a man could possibly be removed, he was sent out to Convalescent Barracks, and when sufficiently able to March, was sent off to join their respective Regiments.

A letter from Plymouth soon after his return records his illness and its lasting effects, and that he had been retained in Plymouth to look after clothing stores before rejoining the Regiment in Colchester.

Too much praise cannot be given to the late General England and Colonel Burnet for their attention to our wants, as also to the laudable part taken by the Inhabitants for the assistance they afforded us in our naked state. Subscriptions were set on foot and largely supported by every one from the Jew to the Prostitute by which means we were again in possession of warm and comfortable Clothing to replace what rags we brought home, which were destroyed to prevent both infection and a circulation of Spanish vermin which were not only numerous but far superior to the British breed in both size and efforts.

It appears to me that every Nation or Kingdom In the Habitable Globe has a peculiar breed of the Animal, Brute and Insect Creation to whom mans partiality is carried so far as nearly to Idolize and Worship, particularly that in the East of the Elephant (the most useful of all Creatures) by the Hindoo.

I shall therefore briefly note them and point them out to your view, having by reason of what I before suggested not been able to give but a short account of Spain, as also being fearful that I may not find sufficient matter to occupy the remaining pages of my book.

The Arabian has his horse. The Egyptian his Camel. The Yankee his Beaver. The Russian his Bear. The Englishman his Dog. The Hanoverian his Cat. The Frenchman his Frog, and the Spaniard his Louse. And what is also remarkable, if those Animals, Brutes or Insects are Removed from its Native place, will not only degenerate and become far less useful, but much inferior in beauty to when it breathed on its primitive soil. For instance, take an English Spaniel, Pointer or Other Dog to Asia, in a very short space of time he will appear as a creature of the Country, loose his sagacity and good Qualifications and to use the language of the Asiatic become a perfect Pariah. The same effect would be, and is produced on the Arabian horse, and perhaps you may say it has had the same effect on myself. It may be so and I shall in concequence of that surmise say no more on this subject as modesty induces me to leave it to a better qualified Zoologyst. Otherwise I might attempt elucidating the whole from the Hindoo and his Elephant to the Spaniard and his Louse.

I joined my Regiment about the middle of April and found them very sickly and many had died, but the arrival of the Spring and good nourishment together with ease from drills and dutys soon brought the greater part about again, when towards the beginning of May another Volunteering from the Militia took place which nearly brought us to our former number.

We left upwards of a hundred men prisoners of War in Spain, but some of whom found means to escape and rejoined the Regiment. I cannot say how many Died or were Killed, but of the former, a great many.

Chapter 8

An Old Soldier
1809 - 1815

Our Regiment recovering from their sickness and a good number of Recruits and Militia Volunteers having joined us, about the beginning of July we began to smell strong of Holland.

A smart Expedition being formed under the Earl of Chatham amongst which we made a part. Our Brigade consisted of the 2nd (Queens), 76th and 84th Regiments having Brigadier Ackland for our Commander Embarked at Harwich and the Downs appointed the Rendezvous, we Embarked about the 10th.

The Walcheren expedition was the largest that up till that time ever been sent out from Great Britain, with over 39,000 troops, 35 line-of-battle ships, 22 frigates, and many smaller vessels.

As this service was in part to be performed by the Navy, we made a grand Appearance leaving England for the Scheldt, where we arrived after a few hours sailing. Our first performance was to gain footing on the Island of Walcherin, which was done with much ease at Ten Vier *[Veere]* a neat little port about 8 miles from Flushing. Having landed we marched through Middleburgh expecting there to meet with opposition, but the Enemy had fled into Flushing and we followed after. Next morning we encamped within about a mile of the Garrison and immediately commenced erecting our Batterys.

Walcheren

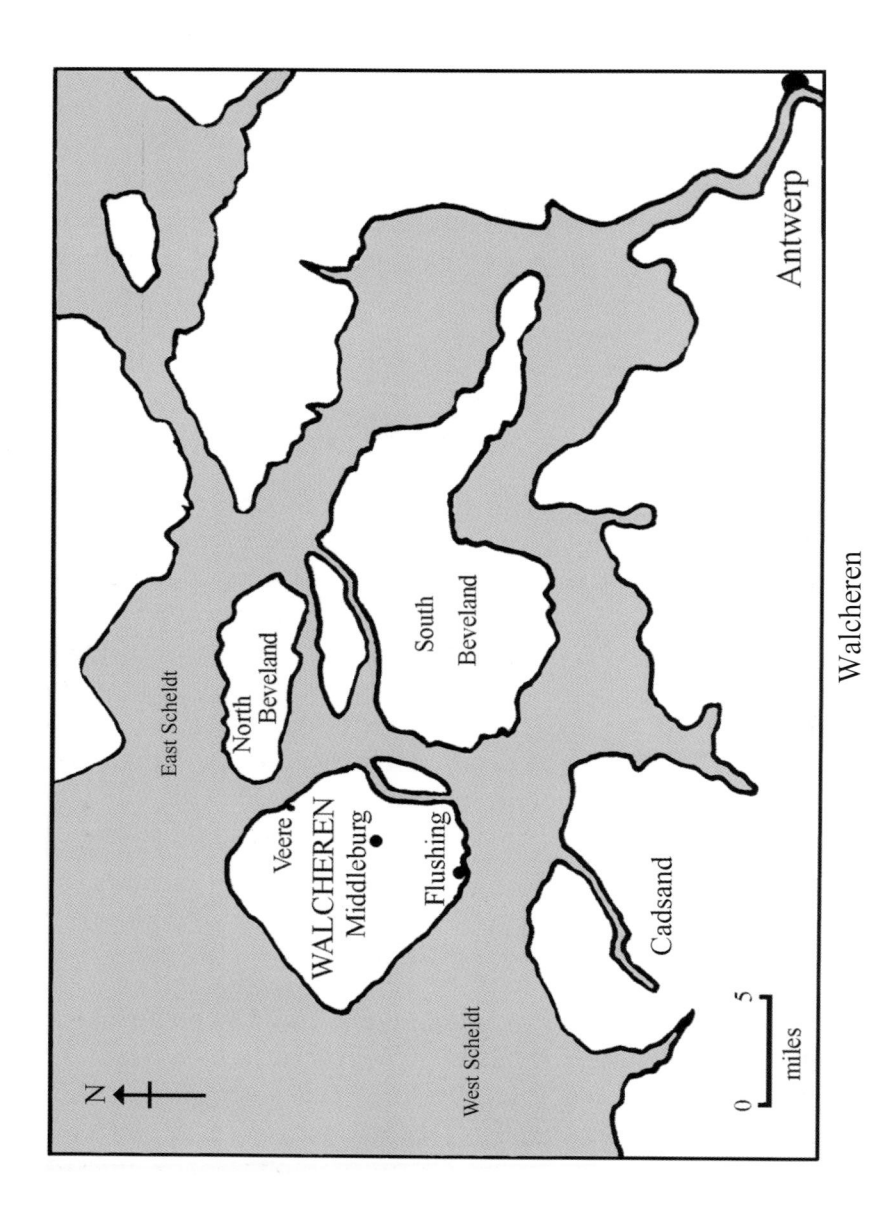

This Siege was conducted with good Skill and Judgement. The Congreave Rockets did much execution and the fireing from the Batterys had great effect from shore and also from the fleet on water, but from our Superiority in number could not claim great praise. The Enemy having attempted in vain to hurt us by turning the water as also by a fruitless sally gave over all hopes of maintaining the Garrison, soon after gave it up and submitted themselves Prisoners of War.

The Regiment, providing pickets on the left flank, only lost two men in this sortie. They were their only casualties to enemy action in the whole campaign.

The Prisoners being Shipped for England, we after leaving a good Garrison in Flushing and Middleburgh and detachments in other places of strength again Embarked intending if possible to get possession of Antwerp towards which we immediately sailed but did not attempt anything. About this time a severe Sickness visited us, which in a day or two induced the General to relinquish his plan of Opperations and return back again to Walcherin when on arrival those intended for its defence landed and the remainder returned to England.

Our Brigade was stationed at Middleburgh where it remained until evacuation of the Island which took place about the Christmas following, leaving a prodigious Number Dead and the survivors little better than Corpses.

By late September the Regiment had 317 men in hospital besides 60 already invalided back to England, and by November it had 107 in hospital and 539 invalided home. In fact the Regiment had almost disappeared, but such as it was, it was one of the last to be evacuated. Three weeks after its return to Ipswich it still had 368 cases of Walcheren fever in hospital. Walcheren fever was primarily malaria, but exasperbated by typhoid, typhus and dysentry, it caused lasting damage. Other contributing factors were the totally incompetent and inadequate medical arrangements, and the squalid, crowded and damp conditions in which the men had to live.

Furthermore the poor provisions for the troops, mainly salt beef and hard biscuit, and the ready availability of spirits, resulted in thirsty men who drank polluted water and ate fruit. It is not surprising that dysentry became rife. The fact that the fatality rate was over 10% for men but only 3% for officers is significant.

There was great public dismay in England and a Parliamentary Inquiry was held into the fiasco. Afterwards Wellington was reluctant to have Walcheren survivors in his army in the Peninsula, due to the long lasting and recurrent effects of malaria.

North and South Beverland (two small Islands also near Walcherin) fell into our hands but from the sickness of the Army also in those Islands together with their little value were not deemed of sufficient concequence to be maintained. The troops were also withdrawn from them.

The Island of Walcherin is a beautiful little spot and the Native Inhabitants remarkably obliging. The Town of Middleburgh (its Capital) is, I think the handsomest I ever saw in Europe of its size, and remarkable clean. It has a navigable Canal through it and is a tolerable Strong Garrison.

There is the greatest difference imaginable among the Inhabitants of this very small Island. The Appearance of Towns people are genteel and polite, but that of the Countryman the most boorish, far exceeding those of Cornwall and Devon in our Country, or even the Natives of Killworth and other mountains in Ireland, but are by far a more harmless and inoffensive people, and was it not for the periodical visitation of its diseases, I think should prefer a residence in it to any place in Europe.

After our return to England we again occupied a part of

the Ipswich Barracks where we remained till the month of May following and then received a Route for Ireland, previous to which, however, I had by Petition obtained leave to be transfered to the 2nd Royal Veteran Battalion then in the Island of Madeira, my state of health requiring a more healthy and temperate climate to recruit itself from the effects of the late Spanish and Dutch Expeditions.

I was not, however, for a considerable time permitted to benefit from the Commander in Chiefs Indulgence in concequence of my being at the time Adjutant Clerk, and returns in concequence of the loss of the Regimental Books and documents Relative to that department far in Arrears was therefore, contrary to wish, under the Necessity of accompanying them to Ireland.

We arrived at the Cove of Cork about the beginning of August and landed at Monkstown. Marched into the Barracks about twelve miles from the place of our landing. Here we remained some weeks and marched to Fermoy a neat little village with good Barracks about 14 miles from Cork where I left them. Finding my health by no means improving and my previous permission neglected, I wrote to Genl Sir Thomas Musgrove our Colonel, who immediately procured me the order for my being forwarded to the Army Depot, Isle of Wight for Embarkation to join my Battalion in the Island of Madeira.

The 76th arrived in Ireland in August 1810, and WK left them in Fermoy later in the year, reaching the Isle of Wight at the end of February 1811, where he stayed, most reluctantly, until the spring of 1813.

The Regiment stayed in Ireland until July 1813, when it went to Spain for the concluding campaign of the Peninsular War. It is ironic that the 75th, after coming home from India only a year after the 76th, and spending a few years on home service, including six months in Horsham in Sussex in 1810/11, were sent to Sicily in 1811, and remained in the Mediterranean for the next twelve years. *No wonder WK regretted leaving the 75th so much.*

On my arrival at the Isle of Wight, I found myself again in an error, no hopes or signs of being sent off appeared for upwards of a year, but what offended me the most was being placed on private pay all the time, after having before received that of Serjeant nearly Twenty Years. All the satisfaction I could receive from my repeated solicitations was that I must be content with the pay of private until joining my Corps in Madeira, when if a vacancy remained I should be paid the difference. This not appearing sufficiently satisfactory to me, I repeatedly applied for leave to be sent off which after about 14 months was complied with and on my joining found there had been seven or eight Serjeants vacant during the whole time but no arrears recoverable, this was the second and last time I was taken in by exchange, but in the end had not reason to complain.

During the greater part of my residence at the Isle of Wight, I was on duty on board the Dido and Buffallo Prison Ships in Cowes river as a Boatswain Serjeant, this duty was the most unpleasant of any I ever performed in any military capacity. The persons there to deal with are the refuse of all Nations. Thieves and Deserters are the most principle. Here they are detained until Opportunity offers of fowarding them to Regiments in the Colonies or perhaps the Hulks. To describe their characters or proceedings would puzzle a Barrington and altho he had a long career in his profession he might find himself here totally outwitted.

HMS Dido was a small frigate that had seen action in the Mediterranean earlier in the war, and the Buffalo had been a naval store ship. Use as a permanently anchored receiving ship or a hulk was often the last stage in a warship's career before being broken up. The prison hulks proper tended to be larger vessels.

George Barrington was a notorious Irish pickpocket who became known as the Prince of Thieves and was transported to Australia in 1790 after a fashionable trial in which he defended himself. He became a Superintendant of Convicts and wrote a memoir about his adventures in 1792. The words
 " True patriots we; for be it understood,
  we left our country for our country's good."
are attributed to him.

We Embarked at Cowes on the 15th of April on the Kate Merchant Brig bound for Bermuda, and after a delightful passage of 12 days arrived in Madeira.

The only Troops doing duty here at this time (exclusive of the Portuguise to whom the Island belongs) were the 2nd Veteran Battalion and two Companys of the Royal Artillery. The Command of the Military Portuguise and English was under Major General Gordon. The Principle Garrisons and Batterys were occupied by the British except the Castle where the Governor resided, which was guarded by the Portuguise.

Madeira is a healthy little Island but unpleasant in other respects.

The Town of Funchal (the only one of any note on the Island) is situate at the Foot of an exceeding high mountain, and the moment you leave the Town you begin ascending them except you go towards the Lhoo fields where you have a tolerable plain for about a mile, in which are some pleasant seats belonging principally to English Merchants. The only thing worthy of Observation is the large Grape plantations and its produce of Wine which is exported to all parts of the world, but in particular to England and both Indies.

This article I expected to find here as cheap as in Spain, but in that I was much deceived for I found the best at the Taverns or retail dealers by the Bottle was a little less price than in England and of inferior quality as a sea voyage is said much to improve it. Beef, Mutton, Pork and Fowles are very scarce and dear particularly when large Fleets arrive. Bread is also very dear and but indifferent. Fish is tolerable plenty but dear also as is everything else except oranges and some other fruits and Rum.

They have a pretty good Cathedrel and some large Friarys as also a tolerable College but it is but little used, except the Chapel attached to it at which the Portuguise Soldiers attend worship on Sundays.

The Natives in general appear to live in a genteel way and do not seem to have many poor among them, at least I did not see any great number of beggars.

The Romish Bishop has a palace but it is a very sorry one indeed to outward appearance altho the inside is not contemptable. I have frequently attended him home after having dined with our General when I have been on duty as his Orderly and allways was presented with a Dollar by him for my trouble, and to do the Portuguise justice I must say they are in general very liberal. I mean those only of this Island.

This Island in former ages is said to have suffered much from Earthquakes but I believe within mans memory this dreadful Calamity has not visited it in any of its dreadful and terrific appearances.

A shock was felt during my residence on it in the month of April but happily did no mischief.

A Rock Fort detached from the Island at the Ponthina (or landing stairs) called the Lhoo Rock, tradition says was seperated from the Island by its cause. It is now surrounded by the sea, and is a great defence to this Island, it having a complete command on all Shiping entering the Roads, here we had a Subaltern Commandant and about 50 men on duty during the residence of the Battalion in Madeira.

About 8 years since, an uncommon fall of Water from the Mountains came down which brought with it stones of great size and weight overflowing the bed of the river, swept away several houses, bridges, and the body of a church, this was considered the more extraordinary as very little rain had fallen at the time to occasion the deluge. Several lives were lost and many had their all carried away with it, since which they have somewhat fortified themselves against the repetition of a similar calamity, should it unfortunately ever occur.

The Portuguise have here a Judge, but his Authority appears to be very limited, all Crimes punishable with death or I believe Transportation are tried at the Brazils to which place both prisoners and Evidences are sent concequently many henious offences are winked at rather than undertake the Voyage to Obtain Justice.

An unfortunate circumstance occured in our Battalion shortly before its return to England which was but ill relished by the Natives.

A Private by the name of Waterson having deranged his intellects through drink, in his Phrensy loaded his Musquet and shot his Serjeant on his bed, the unfortunate man survived but a few hours. The prisoner was tried by a General Court Martial and sentenced to be hanged, which the Portuguise Governor and Inhabitants endeavoured to prevent, it being the only execution which had for numbers of years taken place, but Genl Gordon (who altho a very humane and excellent Character) would not suffer himself to be prevented from making an Example, so very necessary to the Garrison and I believe he went so far as to say that if the Portuguise were after guilty of the like crime or attempt a rescue, they might depend on the same Fate. Be it as it would the execution took place, but not without some Murmurs at encroaching upon the Priveleges of the Island, perhaps thinking that if once this was admitted it might afterwards effect themselves for altho they do not stick at murder, they are no way partial to hanging. And I am convinced the General himself was as averse to it as themselves was it not really necessary to deter others from commiting the same horrid Offence.

In the month of August this year accounts reached us of Lord Wellingtons Victory over the French at Vittoria, which caused great rejoicing amongst all classes of people on this

Island. Illuminations, Fire de joie and thanksgiving in the Catholic Cathedral numerously attended. The service was performed by the Bishop on which occasion some well executed Music on the Organs were introduced with good effect on the Attendants. Shortly after this accounts of Peace reached us from which moment we remained in suspence, dayly expecting the Order for withdrawing the British Troops from the Island. This arrived about the middle of September, when the Bombay Man of War appeared in sight as convoy to five Transport Vessels to convey the Troops and Stores from Madiera.

This Embarkation caused me some trouble and considerable uneasiness, being Store Serjeant to the Garrison, in concequence of the want of Boats to embark the Commissariat Stores, but by considerable exertions the greater part were embarked by the 1st of October, such as could not was left in charge of the English Consol, Mr Veitch.

We Embarked on the 3rd following and sailed the same night, but the Portuguise Governor, Bishop, and principle Gentlemen of the Island having provided a farewell Dinner to the General and his Staff together with most other superior Officers of the Army and Navy did not attempt making way until Evening of the following day, when all being on board, received and returned a Royal salute and parted seemingly to the satisfaction of both Nations.

We had an unpleasant passage home, the months of October and March being generally unfavourable weather in this part of the Ocean, but met with no serious misfortune, and were sufficiently provisioned and watered for a much longer passage. We anchored at Spithead on the 5th Nov where we expected to Disembark, but in concequence of the number of troops lately returned, and continuing to return from the Continent, were ordered round to Chatham and after landing marched into Barracks.

Our arrival within these walls brought to my mind the greater part of the passages of my life, being the first and last

Barracks I was doomed to enter and what is somewhat remarkable the very room out of the many in this large Garrison was the very one in which after an Absence of exactly Twenty Six years I was again to occupy to close my Military service, and being probably the only survivor of the 110 who left England with me for India in 1788.

We landed about the Middle of November, in dayly expectation of receiving the Order for disbandment, being the only Battalion of Veterans remaining on the Establishment, when this arrived we were marched to London and quartered in the Suburbs where we remained till Discharges were prepared. Arms and Stores delivered over and appeared before the board of Commissioners for Chelsea Hospital on the 25th Day of January 1815, where every man of the Battalion whose services entitled him to receive a pension, there received it in advance with an allowance to subsist their Wives and Children home, if they had any.

WK's sergeant's pension, after twenty-six years of hard service amounted to 2s 4 1/2d. a day. There was of course no annual increase for inflation in those days.

I have now, kinsmen, given you a brief narration of the principle occurences of my life, so far as connected with the Military, omitting, however, some circumstances bordering on the Marvelous, which might have been considered not only improbable but Fabulous; or perhaps unlikely and impossible, and conclude with adding thanks to my King and Country for the hard earned benefits I now in an advanced age enjoy, but more particularly to the Almighty disperser of events for protecting and guiding me through the many intricate roads and dark passages between Chatham and Chelsea, the distance however short taking me upwards of twenty five Years to accomplish, and to end as I began shall only add, that should you receive any amusement in reading it as also to pass away an Idle hour, you will be equally rewarded in reading, as I am in writing of it.

    Wm. Kenward
    Lewes   20 December 1815 & following days of 1816.

Coincidentally, only a couple of months after WK's discharge, his one-time guardian Uncle William died, aged 79. In his will WK came into a significant inheritance, which enabled him to live out his days in Lewes quite comfortably, taking lodgings in West Street. He was obviously by then a senior and respected member of the family. This period of the family's history is well documented in letters, wills and the Barkham Manor Court records. WK's own will, made in 1825, makes interesting reading as he was the owner of a house and a number of pieces of land in and around Piltdown. He made considerable money bequests to relations as well as the land. His sister Jane Diplock was his executor, his brother John having already died.

*   Whatever disagreements he had with his family were obviously long forgotten.*

*   The memoir book itself appears to have been in the possession of the Diplock family in Fletching for more than one generation before returning to Barkham and the Kenward family, when it was probably reunited with the surviving letters.*

The area around Fletching

Letters Home

These letters were nearly all sent to William Kenward's elder brother John (JK), who was the head of the family and lived at Moons Farm, Piltdown, which is part of Fletching parish. Letter 2 was written to Mr Isard, his old apprentice master at East Grinstead. His correspondence with John was obviously not all one way, as he did receive some news from home, although complaining frequently that his brother was a poor correspondent. He obviously believed that the rest of the family still thought of him as a n'er-do-well and a black sheep, something which evidently troubled him greatly for a long time, and there is an increasingly fatalistic tone to the letters. However he remained very attached to his family, and sought their news avidly. It would seem from the letters that his first visit home was not until Christmas 1806, nearly twenty years after he left under a cloud.

It is unfortunate that only a fraction of the correspondence has survived and of this some letters have been attacked by mice, as they often contain interesting detail that was not included in the memoirs. Details of addresses have been included where relevant.

Letter 1
WK to JK   Cannanore October 3 1792

Dr. Hond. Brother
   This comes with my Duty to you and the Rest of my Brothers and Sisters and Likewise my Uncle and Aunt & I hope god will

reward them for what they have done for me and I hope you are all well & Happy and enjoy peace and Happiness which we until now have not since I have been in India but I am very happy that the War is now over I hope we shall soon be ordered home for I am tired of this Country for it is a very Unhealthy Place but I thank God for this two years past I have had my health Very Well but was very ill for the 1st year after landing. It would surprise you if you knew the number of Europeans that Die in this country out of One hundred and Ten men which Embarkd. and landed with me only Thirty are now living which was Chiefly owing to the hard fatigues we have had during the War but we had not many killed and now it is all Over I hope we shall have better Times until we return to Europe which I hope will be very soon for a soldiers life is at the best but a poor life Although our pay and Company Allowance is a great deal better than at home but I should be glad to *[be free]* of it and what I have had of it will be a great Service to me for now I have seen my Folly I have not time to write much more at Present but am Suprisd. that I have never heard from you. I hope you will not forget in Particular to remember me to my Sisters Jane and Mary who I am Dayly thinking of and I hope to hear by you that they are both Married and live & Happy & I hope by the Blesing of God soon to see you but I may thank God for my Existance now as I have seen so many strong men fall but as the Scriptures say The Race is not to the swift nor the battle to the strong but Time & Chance Happenth to us all. I hope you will write to me the first Opportunity for I long to hear from you supose I never see you.

         I am your Affectionate Brother
            Wm. Kenward
    Please to direct for
      Wm. Kenward Soldier
      75 Highland Regt.
        Bombay or elsewhere
         East Indies

Letter 2
WK Sergt 75th Regt to Mr Isard at Grinstead

Montana, in the Colichi
Malabar
East Indies
24 Sept 1801

Sir

    I have often thought of writing to you to acquaint you I am in the land of the living which I suppose my Brother did not fail to inform you of.

    I had a letter from him about three months ago acquainting me he was alive, etc. but little more worth Notice except the Death of my Brother Edward which I was before informed of & Sorry to hear, he told me also of Mr Gurrs failing, the loss of my Legacy etc. and gave me a hint of its being Owing to my Own Conduct that I did not receive it as well as himself; all this I must acknowledge to be true but I followed the bent of my own Inclination and I do not repent it. I have been now going on 13 years in India and if God be pleased hope to end my days in it. I never wish to see England any more. The Rgte. I have Served in since I have been in the Army is a very good one, have also distinguished themselves at different times in action and I think myself no disgrace to them and certain I am the Army is no disgrace to me.

    I have received no Injury as yet God be praised by wounds or any other disorders incident to the Country but remain in good health and peace of mind. We have been in the field now going on three years and but little prospect of leaving it. The petty Rajahs of the Country have since the capture of Seringm. and Death of Tippoo been in a state of Rebellion, but are paying dear for their Conduct. We have lost a good many men nevertheless by the Rajah of Colichi who we are now Employed against but I believe it is nearly all over, as he is entirely deserted by his own men & now is Oblidged to conceal & Disguise himself & reported to be in miserable condition in the woods, where we cannot as yet have the good fortune to discover his retreats.

The Polygars a desperate set of Robers are also at war with us, the 74th and 77th Regts. have suffered hard by them and we Expect so soon as the weather and other circumstances will admit to march and join them.

We have also an Army from this Country gone to Egypt under command of General Baird an Experienced Officer, the same who lead us on to victory at the Storm of Seringapatam on the 4 May, and several Field actions Previous to it if possible more Brilliant.

My Brother wrote me word that he Expected me to have made a fortune on that day but if he had been with me he would have seen other business to Employ himself about besides Plundering.

I have wrote three letters within this few months to him which you will oblidge me by Informing him of and please remember me to my uncles & aunts Brothers & Sisters, Mrs. Isard your son & Daughters, Mr. Thomas and all who know me at Grinstead. I shall always be happy to hear from home should any one think me worth writing to. If not I shall content myself with never sending a letter past the Cape of Good Hope after this for I have sent 40 Home which I have never received answer from.

No more but remain

Hond. Sir, Yrs Obedly.

WK

This letter was sent to Mr. Isard at East Grinstead, WK's old apprenticemaster, so it would seem that the "predal act" which he gives in the memoirs as the reason for running from his apprenticeship was indeed not all that heinous. However we are unlikely ever to discover exactly what it was. Perhaps a young man's boredom also had something to do with it. How this letter came to be with those sent to his brother is unclear. Possibly 'the G......s failing" refers to the Golder or Gelder family who are mentioned often in later letters. It is also possible that the lost legacy was from this family, as, in view if the generosity of his Uncle William when he died, it does not seem to be a Kenward family legacy.

It is interesting that, only five years after saying that he never wanted to see England again, he took the major step of transferring to another regiment so that he could come home.

Letter 3
WK Sergt.75th Reg to JK at Moons   (In Gujerat)
(many parts of letter missing)   ca Apr 1803

....

I beg of you not to allow yourself to be so much Afflicted for a Prodigal brother. My roving disposition Dear Brother would not I am sensible allow me was I now in England to remain at home, & why should you desire of me to perform Impossibilites. But you may believe me my regard for you all is truly sincere & you in particular I have much to heart. I am also sensible of the great & many Obligations I owe to my Uncle as also the duty I owe to my friends in general.

You seem to suppose my reasons for not wishing to return to England again is owing to my being married, which is also Mrs Diplocks oppinion that is not at present the case. Marriage is not very common in India the Native Women here will take a mans word for the performance of his duty rather than trouble a minister. This I dare say you will not approve off & I cannot say very much in favour of it myself. But it is allmost as rare to see a Parson in India as it is to see a Shower of Snow & that is more than I have seen this 13 years............

.... Stationers Shop in London or I dare say in the Country. If not by addressing a note "To the Officer Commanding H.M .36 Regt." he will most probably receive an answer.

However I am off Opinion it will be useless as a great part of the 36 Regt. when ordered home went to the 76th Regt and are in Bengal some thousands of miles from where I now am but should us ever meet I will make every inquiry & will not fail to acquaint you for Mr Chapmans Information.

 Since my last writing to you we have been much harased & Fatigued; after Subduing the rebels I formerly wrote about. A Dispute happened between two Mahratta Chiefs and as is common, the weak side applied to the Government of Bombay for assistance. The 75th & 84th regts. werein consequence Embarked, on the 20th February last and after an unpleasant passage of 14 days landed here and marched to the place in question which is called Keria about 120 miles from this were we arrived on the 9th March. On the 31st by daybreak we commenced an action with them and after 5 hours hard work they finding us in possession of most of their Guns & Batteries Surrendered the Garrison but not until they had lost a great Number of Men in Killed & Wounded - & we suffered allso pretty considerable loss but not so much as might have been supposed considering that we were Exposed to the whole fire of the Garrison of ….. & grape shot and also a number of Batteries that Played smartly on us the whole time. I myself was within an Inch of loosing my right leg by a 12 Pound shot which I have reason to thank god just took off the skin & did me no more injury than a few minutes pain, it did not prevent me from doing my duty & I have scarcely a mark now left. I should if I had Paper left have given you a more full account but I am affraid you ….. not like the subject & ………….Drops it.

 Do let me persuade you Dear Brother ………….self so much trouble on account of me. I am …………….want of nothing & I was I have many friends …………..more (but not so dear) as in England. I am……………...…… the whole regiment from the Major Commanding …………..Black Cooks. My Duty to God I hope…………….omit my duty to my King I dare

not............you wrote me word in Chatham As I made my bed I must lye on it. I must also say that I have not any desire of changing my present situation which is that of a Soldier. No more fm. Yr. Affectionate brother
WK

I hope you can read this, if not, I cannot write more plain Give my love & Duty to all my brothers & sisters also my uncle & aunts and all acquaintances & friends.
Direct as formerly Bbay or Else………..

Presumably Mrs Diplock was his sister Jane, the landlady of the Griffin Inn at Fletching. Despite WK's comments about native women not bothering about formal marriage vows, the fact that one managed to follow her man all the way back to Colchester, much to his consternation, showed how faithful they could be. See Letter 19.

It is interesting that he does not mention in the actual memoirs how close he was to a likely fatal injury when a cannon ball grazed his leg during this engagement, although he mentions it to his brother.

Letter 4
WK to JK at Moons   On board the Ship Lady Castlereagh
off Scilly
July 17th 1806

Dear Brother
I have just time to acquaint you of my arrival this far, and hope in a few days to be on shore, but cannot say at what place we may disembark. The boat which takes this on shore is waiting. When we land I will write more fully till then Adieu
Yr Affect. Brother
WK

Letter 5
WK to JK at Moons, Fletching.
                                                           Dartford Kent
                                                           24 July 1806

Dear Brother,

   I wrote you a few lines some days ago from the Castlereagh Indiaman off the Lands End but on account of the hurry of the departure of the boat I had only time to say that on Landing I would write to you again.

   I now sit down to acquaint you that I am well and hearty as ever I was in my life God be praised for it. I hope you and all the family are in the same state.

   We left Bengal on the 17th February and proceed to Point de Gaul, on the Island of Ceylon, where we watered and being joined by the Bombay and Madras Ships, we sailed again from there on the 16th March and arrived at Saint Helena on the 20th May and after remaining for a few days to water the shipping sailed again for England, where we landed yesterday near Gravesend.

   I dare say you are surprised to hear of my return to England and more so with the 76th Regt. Having exchanged from the 75th who are only I dare say by this time leaving India, but as the 75th will when they arrive most probably proceed direct to Scotland I thought it most advisable to return with an English regiment.

   The 75th did indeed land at Leith the next year.

   How long we may remain in England God knows, we must be a considerable time before we are completed, having scarcely a man fit for duty (Non-commissioned Officers excepted). The Regiment was weak before, and when the order arrived for proceeding home all who were able prefered staying in India and Joined other Corps some in the Kings and some in the Companys service as they thought best. The Sergeants Corporals Drums and Band were not allowed to remain in India, or otherways there would he scarcely a man to come home with the Colours except those who have lost limbs, a great many of whom are now come home disabled in the last Campaign in Hindoostan. I thank God I have escaped the last Campaign, as well as all others which was indeed the severest I have ever seen in India.

As we left India nearly in peace most probably there will be a many regiments returning to England these some years to come, they having been a great many years abroad, but none now remaining but the 19th Light Dragoons who have been out so long as ourselves except the 75th and 77th who are now under orders to proceed home.

I hope you will not be long in answering this as I am anxious to hear how you all do, and hope I shall soon have the pleasure of seeing you all well and then I dont care a farthing how soon I leave England again should the war continue.

I wrote to you by an invalid of the 75th when we was at Fort William acquainting you of the Regiment having left the Bombay Establishment. I should like to know whether you received it or not. Bengal is by far the most beautiful country of the two and more rich and fertile, but nothing near so healthy. The Hot Winds carries off great Numbers every season.

Both the 75th and 76th suffered very severely by the last campaign as well as all other Regiments who were present at the Siege of Burtpore by three attempts to storm the place all of which failed in Consequence of the Garrison being surrounded by water, of a great width and depth, but the Rajah Capitulated with Lord Lake who was determined at all events to take it and his son as Hostage for the performance of the Treates.

Marquis Cornwallis was about 500 miles from Calcutta by the upper provinces when he died; I saw his grave which is at a place called Gazipure on the banks of the river Ganges.

Never was man more regreted than his Lordship by all ranks of men, and particularly by the Natives of India. Lord Lake also is greatly respected (except by our enemies) he is a most Excellent General, and adored by the Army.

I must now come to a conclusion beging to be remembered to all Brothers Sisters and relations, and all such as you know of my old acqaintances and friends now living and remain with the greatest regard

Dr Brother Yr etc
WK

Letter 6
WK to JK at Moons   Covent Garden London
12 August 1806

Dear Brother

    I received yours this morning and was much concerned by not hearing from you sooner however as I was not present with the Regt. when it arrived it was brought to me to day only here.

    I am sorry to say I am disappointed in my expectations of coming to see you at present but hope to get permission some time during the summer.

    I am here with the Adjutant and Paymaster of the Regt. settling with Invalided men now at Chelsea after that I must go on to Nottingham which is to be the Headquarters of the Regiment and where we shall remain sometime.

    If any one coming this way of my acquaintance shall stop at Charing Cross (which is the place most of the Stages stop at) within these few days I shall be happy to see them, but none so much as yourself. However it would be useless for you to come up at present as it is only chance how many days I may stop here.

    The Adjutant gave me his word should have a furlow soon after our arrival at Nottingham and as he is my friend I can have no reason to doubt it, having been but seldom disappointed by an Officer.

    I am much concerned to hear of the deaths you mentioned, but we must all pay the same debt sooner or later. Give my best

respects to all friends , and must conclude in Haste & remain yr Obedt. Brother
WK

Letter 7
WK Sergt 76 Regt. to JK.   Nottingham 27 August 1806

I wrote to you from London about the 13th or 14th lastly. I was there then on business which prevented me from answering the letter you sent to me at Dartford. I suppose you could not have received it as the Regt. left Dartford on the 11th and arrived here on the 21st where we may expect to remain for some time as we have as yet very few recruits as yet joined the Regiment but we are getting some dayly.

I am happy to hear you are well as also all our relations, but I am sorry to hear of the deaths you mentioned. I was such in hopes of obtaining leave of absence before now, but was prevented from it by being with the Adjutant and Paymaster of the Regt. I could not then be spared but am promised as soon as ever we get a little settled to have some leave.

I hope you will not fail to answer this as soon as possible as I expected to hear from you again before this but I suppose you are busy with your harvesting. Give my respects to all relations and acquaintances who are in life and I hope to see them before long.

I remain dr Brother
WK

Letter 8
WK to JK at Moons   Nottingham 10 September 1806

Dear Brother

    I received yours dated the 5th the day before yesterday and applied for a furlow afterwards thinking that now us we are getting a little settled to have it granted. My answer was that I was certainly deserving it and that all Indulgence that could be given to a man was no more than I could claim or expect, but the present want of people to do the business of the Adjutants office could not be had amongst all the recruits etc we have received here. We therefore content ourselves until more favourable opportunity offers of meeting if it may ever happen.

    I am sorry I did not remain with the 75 until they arrived I might then have been certain of what I was promised by the Officer who am now with which was that I should have a furlow as soon as I required after arriving in England. We are getting recruits fast here I wish we may be soon filled up. If I cannot get leave to come down in the Course of the year sometime, my determination is to write to his Royal Highness the Duke of York, and am sorry when I was at the Horse Guards in London I did not do it then. The Colonels Lt Colonels or Major are not here otherwise I should not have any great trouble in procuring what I want.

        No more but I remain your loving Brother
                              WK

PS   Give my best regards to all enquiring friends.
      You need not be at the expense of paying the Postage of your letters. All they can charge me is One penny to any part of the Globe.

Letter 9
WK Sergt 76 Regt to JK at Moons   Mansfield 15 Nov 1806

Dear Brother
    It is a long while now since I have heard from you. From my last which I wrote about a month ago I have received no answer, I hope you are not sick or what else can present you from writing more frequently.
    We are now removed to Mansfield on account of the Election at Nottingham which we expect will finish this day or tomorrow at furthest, when we shall return again to our former station and I dare say we shall remain at Nottingham this year or two. We are now wanting upwards of 550 men to complete us.
    I shall have a furlow as soon as Colonel Monson arrives from Lincoln where he is gone for the purpose of the Election and is returned from that place. We may therefore expect him dayly.
    We hear from Nottingham dayly that place is in great confusion on account of their new members. I suppose about you there is no much opposition. Give my respects to all friends and hoping all relations etc enjoy good health remain
              yrs etc etc etc
                  WK

Letter 10
WK to JK   Lincoln 4th February 1807

Dear Brother,
    I arrived at this place on the Evening of the 1st instant, and left London at 5 o' clock on the 31st. We had a very cold and snowy night indeed but thank God I have received no harm by it.
    We have not got many recruits since I have been away. 253 privates is all we have got as yet but the greatest part of the Regiment is now out a'recruiting.

The Adjutant told me I might have stayed as much longer as I pleased so that I was back in time to prepare the Books and Returns for the Inspecting General who will see us in the beginning of the next month and then no man must be Absent. He was writing a letter to send to me the night I arrived here to acquaint me of it.

The frost here seems to be set in for some time. I dont think it is so sharp downwards, but your weather glass can tell better than I can Judge.

Give my best respects to all friends relations and Acquaintances & shall be glad to hear from you frequently.

I am rather hurried at present therefore you will Excuse my saying no more but remain etc etc
WK

Letter 11
WK to JK at Fletching Lincoln 16 February 1807

Dear Brother

I wrote to you a few days after my return here agreeable to my promise when I left Fletching, But not having received any answer I fear the letter must not have arrived, and as I thought you would be surprised at my not writing, should that have been the case I have taken the opportunity of again writing to inform you that I arrived safely at Lincoln on the 1st Instant after a very disagreeable and Cold ride of 25 hours from London.

I have nothing worth relating to inform you of. We recruit still but slowly. The day before yesterday we were Inspected by General Thornton from Hull who was pleased to say that we appeared much to his satisfaction.

In Addition to the Priviledge allready granted to the Regiment by his Majesty of wearing the word <u>Hindoostan</u> in our Colours and other appointments The Elephant is also added as a proof of

His Majesty's approbation of the services of the Regiment abroad.

    I wish my old Regt. was back to see what would be granted them as honorary Distinctions they have also dearly earnt it.

    I am sorry to say my old friend the adjutant is going to leave us. He has got Captain in the German legion, Count Frobergs Regiment, now stationed in the Mediterranean, and he says he shall leave Lincoln in three weeks or less. He is particulary anxious to get me promotion if it is ever in his power, and says that also Colonels Morgan and Macrae will support my interest if I had any friends of Rank in my own Country to forward it etc.

    We shall leave Lincoln about the 5th or 6th March next for a week or ten days as the Assizes commence on the 7th March for Gainsbro or Newark which is a few miles distant after which we shall again return to Lincoln.

    I hope Couzin Diplock continues recovering and that you are all as well as when I left you. I thank God I am quite well.

    Give my duty and respects to all friends and relations not forgetting Mr & Mrs Gilder also the Isards if you should see them.

and conclude Yr Affectionate Brother
                      WK

PS If you have not allready wrote I hope you will not fail answering this as I shall always be Happy to hear how you all do.

Letter 12
WK Sergt 76 Regt to JK at Moons   Lincoln 18 March 1807

Dear Brother
    Yours dated 14th I received yesterday and am happy you all continue well as I thank God this leaves me. I am concerned for the death of Brother Robert but hope he is gone to a much better

world which sooner or latter we must all do.

I an extremely sorry that Brother Robert .... did not let me know about a fortnight ago, and what you mentioned should have been at his service, but previous to our march to Gainsbro' to which we went during the Assizes I put it in the hands of a Gentleman for fear of loosing it on the march and I fear it will not be agreable to him to let me have it out again Immediately, after asking him to favor me as to do it for me, he is to give me 5 1/2 per cent.

I still remain as formerly, the late Adjutant went to join his Regt. during our Stay at Gainsborough and have at present no Adjutant but expect dayly to have one appointed who he is no one knows as yet, but I much fear we shall never get the like of the last.

I do not think it worth while to trouble our heads about getting anything done in regard to Preferment I am comfortably situated and what more is desirable.

I am happy to hear our Cousin Diplock still keeps recovering the summer will I hope be beneficial to him.

We have three men to suffer death at this place to morrow convicted at the late Assizes.

I have nothing more to add but beg my kind remembrances to all Brothers Sisters Uncles aunts relations and enquiring friends not forgetting Mr & Mrs Golder and my old master and family if you should go the E Grinstead ways.

    I remain your ever affectionate brother
              WK

PS   I should like to know who made you a f...................
I dont think you could have made one since I left you if you have soon recovered of the operation. You had better go to Lewes they will perhaps tell you the meaning of your ...... I dont think but Mr Westerson the Barber can if he chooses however I never spoke to him about it.   WK

Letter 13
WK Sergt 76 Regt. to Mrs Jane Diplock, Griffin Inn, Fletching.

Lincoln 14 June 1807

Dear Sister

I wrote my brother yesterday at which time I Acquainted him that I expected we should remain some time here. We have just now received an Order to proceed to the Island of Jersey and are to commence our march on Monday morning next the 15th. Instant. From what port we are to Embark we are not yet informed but most probably from Portsmouth.

Let the fortune of war direct me to any part of the Universe you may rest assured that I shall for ever regard you with the sincerest affection and esteem, and shall for ever bear in remembrance Brother Diplock & Children, my uncle & aunt and all friends & relations.

I remain Dear Sister, Yr Affe brother

WK

Letter 14
WK Sergt. 76 Regt to JK Fletching

St Heliers, Jersey
27th July 1807

This being the first opportunity I have been able to embrace since landing on this Island of acquainting you of my good state of health for which God be thanked, and hope this will find you all in the same state. We embarked at Spithead and saild on the 5th Inst. landed here on the 9th, where expect to remain some time. We were near having the bottom of our ship destroyed thro the ignorance of the Pilot when close to the Island, happily the weather was fair and had the vessel sunk we should have had a fair chance of escaping among the many rocks which surrounds this small but beautiful island.

The Peace concluded between France Russia etc will make

us here allways alert, and cause many extraordinary duties which we were not accustomed to in England but what some few of us have before experienced abroad in a simpler degree.

I cant say that at present I am in any way partial to this place but must say that it is at this season of the year beautiful beyond description and most things cheaper than in England particularly all Contriband goods. The free Exportation & Importation of what is allowed being a free Island. Consequently Tea Tobacco Rum Gin etc etc etc is allmost given away; Bread beef etc much the same as in England but inferior in quality.

We Expect (by a report of an Officer of ours recruiting at Hull in Yorkshire) to get some Volunteers from the Sussex Militia. Many of whom should they be permitted, <u>which it is expected they will be</u>, would now join us, I shall then perhaps find some old acquaintance.

The dread of the insuing winter is the only object I have at heart, as allso many of our old hands, some of whom are determined to Petition for leave to proceed to India or some other warm climate.

Should any of you wish for a short sea trip I could not recommend a more pleasant one than to this Island a few days would bring you from Sussex to Jersey and I am persuaded that it would answer many complaints disorders better than employing a doctor and also be attended with less expense.

Give my dutiful respects to my uncle and aunt Brothers and Sisters ……and…….. all Couzins relations and friends. Particularly our Couzins at Uckfield, acquaintances at Barkham, Mr Gelder etc etc etc and remain dear Brother,
      yours Affectionately
      WK

Excuse the rough scroll, the Packet is to sail this Evening or tomorrow morning, therefore I am in haste to return this in the Post Office fearing it might have to remain till next Conveyance.
   Direct to me as before   Grenville Barracks Jersey

Letter 15
WK Sergt. HM 76th to JK Fletching   Jersey 3 September 1807

Dear Brother

Yours of date 14 August I received on the 28th last and am happy to hear of your health, the increase of Sister Diplocks family; your prosperous harvest etc. but am sorry to hear at the same time that my uncle and Couzin Diplock are still unwell.

We are in this island in a state of anxious hopes of having an Opportunity of trying what our young Battalion can do with Monsieur Bounaparte, from St Maloes twelve or more vessels seemingly large can be plainly perceived and Signals are now flying on the Island signifying the same, and supposed to be designed for this Island. We are however well prepared to receive them and nothing would give us more pleasure than a game of Bowles with them.

The Natives of this Island are rather daunted but are all as one, determined should that be the case to make a firm resistance.

We are here well supplied with news from England. The Pacquet generally arrives twice a week therefore you can have no excuse for not writing frequently.

We have not heard as yet how our parties got on with the Militia in regard to volunteers. Then Officers certainly will use their utmost endeavours to procure as many as possible. Should they be able to raise a few hundreds we shall most probably form a Second Battn. which will of course cause considerable promotion among them.

Please give my dutiful respects to my Uncle and Aunt Sisters brothers Couzins and all friends and acquaintances. I hope Mrs Golder is still in health.

                I remain Dr Brother
                Yrs Effectionately
                    WK

Letter 16
WK HM 76 to JK at Maltster etc Fletching   Grenville Barracks
Jersey
17 October 1807

Yours of date 6th October I received on the 13th which gave me great pleasure and satisfaction to hear you were all in good health. We have nothing passing here at present all is dull. We have received 90 Volunteers from West Middlesex Militia and more are Expected every day to arrive from the different Regiments from England, we expect to be Completed to our Establishment in a short time, and most probably shall then leave this Island for Foreign Service.

You wished to know what number of troops we have here. The Regts. at present stationed on the Island are the 57th 58th 76th 90th, 4th Garrison Battalion and a Battn. of Veterans which in all I suppose would amt. to 4 thousand men besides the Militia of the Island, every man whereof is in possession of Arms and is duly trained up to them. Consequently we could not be at any great loss to defend ourselves should that be the wish of our opposite Neighbours to put to a trial.

We expect to have a number of Regts. from England shortly and it would not be any wonder after that we was to return again to England as they seldom keep regiments here for any long period.

Be good enough to give my dutiful respect to my uncle and aunt and all brothers sisters friends relations and acquaintances
& believe me I remain with sincere regard
Your ever Obedt. Brother
WK

I hope you do not forget to remember at Barkham, Mr Gelders, and at Uckfield also Couzin Diplocks & Mr Isards, as I always wish in particular agreeable to their requests to let them know how I remain.

Letter 17
WK Sergt 76th to JK at Moons   Jersey 20th January 1808

Dear Brother

  Some time having elapsed since I wrote to you in consequence of dayly expecting to leave this Island for England, no such order having yet been received I write wishing you all a happy new year.

  We most assuredly shall be in England this next Spring but I imagine for the purpose of some Expedition (Perhaps South America) as we learn (another) <u>and I hope more successful than the last will be sent to Buenos Aires.</u>

  We have no news here excepting that this and Guernsey Islands will be allowing a few days to trade with France in vessels not exceeding 100 Tons Burthen, consequently this & Guernsey will be considered neutral, and the troops from hence withdrawn, and which in my simple opinion has a view of peace.

  We receive our new Colours at St Heliers Church on the 26th Inst. They are extremely Grand, a Sermon will be preached on the occasion.

  We have a report here of the Prize Money being about to be paid, for the captures of Colombo Pondicherry & Seringapatam all of which I am entitled to, I will thank you to enquire thro our Couzin at Uckfield from Mr Chase if he has any information from his Brother Peter on the subject and if in fact he receive it for me. Should Mr Chase give you this information, he will be able to direct you where it is receivable.

                I remain Dr Brother
                yrs Affectionately
                      WK

I hope my uncle & aunt Brothers Sisters friends & relations are still well and have enjoyed a merry Christmas. I should be happy to hear from Mr and Mrs Gelder.

In another hand (JK's?):
>Colombo Prize Money Payable
>at Mr Jackson's Broad street City
>Pondichery Not yet Payable
>Seeringapotam Prize money apply to
>David Scott & Co London on account of Tulloch
>& Co at Madras

Letter 18
WK Sergt. 76 Regt to JK at 'Mr Wm Kenwards', Moons
>Jersey   18 March 1808

  I received yours dated the 1st inst by the last pacquet a few days ago. Previous to which I had wrote to Mr Isard at East Grinstead fearing you were not well or prevented by some unavoidable cause. I am truly sorry our uncle still remains poorly but hope the approaching Spring may benefit him. The remainder of our friends and relations you inform are well which I rejoice to hear.

  I am greatly oblidged to Couzin Kenward for her inquiry but I fear my letter has not been understood - the prize money I meant was for Seringapatam – whether the 2nd Payment was made - the first I received myself Six years or nearly ago, the 2nd when paid I have to receive 3 shares….. two being what I was allowed me as Sergt and one for a deceased comrade by Will. For Colombo third payment which was expected to be paid when we left India I have two shares by Will - the 1st and 2nd payments for Colombo were paid a considerable while ago. For Pondicherry should it ever be paid I have the same. I made the Prize Rolls myself before I left the 75th but they inform me they was not paid in India.

  I shall write to the 75th again in a few days from whom I shall receive the requisite information and as I am included in their rolls I suppose from them (as they are now at home) I may receive the payment or an Order on the Agents to that purpose when payable. I shall write to you again on receiving their answer.

We expect soon to be in England and as we are informed we shall go to Colchester in Essex I shall perhaps he able to see you before we leave it which is supposed will not be long as we supposed ourselves to be amongst the first regiments for foreign I shall not much regret leaving this Island the winter has been severe and firing scarce. The cold weather pinches me now as much as ever, I was in hopes last winter would have seasoned me to it.

I wish you would inform me in your next if Brother & Sister Haver keep the house at Newick and how they get on. I hope Couzin Diplock's Complaints have left him.

We have had of late a great number of our Noncommissioned Officers & Privates discharged and pensioned and more are the next Inspection expected. I am now amongst the oldest in the Regt but have no chance of expecting it some years to come as I am still employed in the Regimental Orderly Room and the Regiment's badly off for Clerks who understand the duty of that office.

Give my dutiful respects to my uncle and aunt Brothers Sisters friends and relations. And remain with sincere regard.
yr. Effecte. Brother
WK

Letter 19
WK Serg 76 Regt to JK at Maltster etc Fletching.   Colchester
28 August 1808

Yours of date the 14th Instant I received on the 16th and thought that would have been the last I should have for some time received from you, but as the times are now so precarious I do not know whether or not we are to proceed at all. The Transports which were arrived for our reception at Harwich have received Counter orders & have sailed nearly this fortnight - and we learn such of the Troops who were to form a part of the Expedition with us, and who had Embarked are again disembarked and gone into their Inspection Quarters.

 A rumour is now in circulation of forces being about to be sent to Guadaloupe in the West Indies, an Island belonging to the French perhaps should that be the case we may be ordered on that Service. Martinico*[Martinique]* has allready given up.

 We are in dayly expectation of having a Second Battn. added to our Regt. Should that be the case a number of the oldest NonCommissioned Officers will be transferred to it for the formation thereof. It will create much promotion with the Officers but none with us, some few Corporals may indeed be promoted to Sergt. and a sergeant might for four or five Hundred pounds get an Ensigncy - The practice of promoting Non Commissioned Officers without purchase seems to have ceased. I wish I had remained till now in India I think I should have had accomplished it by this time.

 If we do not proceed in a month or two it is most likely we shall not the season will be too far advanced for any Expedition after, for this Winter. And hence we will most likely remain perishing with cold - Colchester is indeed a nice place enough and articles reasonable, but I had much rather have had proceeded to Portugal or Spain or indeed any were else so it was not to a cold Climate.

 I have read in the papers of the same fleet of Indiamen having returned to England safe again, and have had two letters from thence. War is still carried on in some part of it but not so serious as formerly.

 We had a black woman in Camp some days which came to England in the last fleet, as waiting woman to some children, she was formerly an acting wife to one of our Regt. who is now in

Camp and little expected to have seen her in this part of the World. She set off for London yesterday in order to proceed by the next fleet to Bengal again.

Give kind remembrance to all whom I formerly mentioned & hope our uncle & Willm. Diplock are mending. Hoping you have had a plentiful Harvest

I remain yr sincere & Effectionate Brother

WK

I hope our Couzins at Uckfield all enjoy good health, to whom do not forget to give my kind remembrance.

Letter 20
WK to JK at Moons   On board the ship Comet off Deal
                                                21 Sept.*[1808]*

Dr Brother

I take this opportunity (perhaps the last for a considerable time to come) of informing you of our embarkation at Harwich on the 12 instant, and should have instantly sailed for the Downs but unfortunately struck on a Sand bank and with difficulty got her off at the next tide, but the wind having become foul we was oblidged to remain until the 20th Morning we have now a promising aspect of a good voyage to a destination yet unknown. It is however generally believed for the North of Spain. You must excuse my not writing more fully for the Confused State we are in prevents me from getting to my paper and with difficulty can find a place to write on but when safely landed will give you a detailed account of all that has happened - as also I hope to be able to add the Hindoostan Regiment having had an opportunity of distinguishing themselves in Europe as well as on the plains from whence they have the honour of wearing that distinctive mark of His Majestys approbation.

I remain with sincere Affection
WK

Give my respects as formerly I hope they enjoy health. You complain of not being able to read my letters. I fear you will find this more than usually dificult, but if you cannot read it yourself someone or other perhaps can. It does not contain treason Heresy nor Scism, therefore you had best do as most of the Highlanders do, <u>take it to the parson of the Parish</u> for explanation.

Letter 21
WK Sergt 76 Hindoostan Regt to JK at Moons.

New Granby Barracks
Plymouth Dock Devon
(*Undated but rec'd 21 March 1809*)

Dr Brother

    I have wrote twice since my being detained here by illness to neither of which you have been kind enough to favour me with answer which makes me uneasy. I shall take it kind of you not to delay answering this as I hope soon to leave Plymouth.

    I have a dangerous feaver but am now sufficiently recovered to Join the Regt. which is at Colchester. Was it not that since my recovery I have been ordered to remain in charge of the Clothing for the men who dayly come from Hospitals but hope soon to be able to quit it as the men are now getting fewer.

    Since my Illness my Eyesight has much failed me and I find myself much the worse man for the Cursed Spanish Expedition, our hardships at times were indescribable but I praise God I was more fortunate than many a brave fellow who fell Victims to Cold Hunger and Captivity. I shall write more fully in my next should I receive an answer.

Till then adieu.

                    Yr Sincere & Effectionate Brother
                                    WK

    I hope you will not forget to give my dutiful respects etc etc as formerly directed.
WK

Letter 22
WK Serg. 76 Hindoostan Regt. to JK at Moons
                        Ipswich Barracks 27 April *[1809]*

        I again take the opportunity of writing a few lines hoping they will find you and all relations well. I am sorry I cannot say I am entirely well myself having laboured under a most painful and dangerous illness. I am however, thank God so far recovered as to be able to join my regiment which is lying here. I arrived here on the 22nd instant and came by the London coach from Plymouth there and also from thence to this place having been requested to join them as soon as possible, the confused state of the Regiment since it leaving Spain requiring every exertion to account for it, left it out of the power of any but myself to arrange which I am now busily employed at. I came free of any charge and was gladly received on my arrival here and every comfort afforded me.
        I have found many alterations and casualties since I have joined, many who were in good health when I left them from on board ship on the last unfortunate Expedition, have died through the fatigues which had attended it, and many others are yet so unwell as not to be able to do any duty, little however is required as there is particular orders for the troops returned from Spain not to do any, and our Commanding Officer pays every attention to the order.
        We have every reason to believe we shall again soon be

ordered abroad as all the army is held in readiness and we are filling up fast from the Militia, - where we may next proceed for God only knows, but I hope to a climate more favourable to a British Constitution than the North of Spain

Great preparations are making in all the Army and all seem anxious for another Campaign. I expect this summer will decide the fate of Portugal & Spain if not Austria whether or not they will become subjects to Buonaparte which I am rather doubtful will be the case, but hope not.

I hope you will take all opportunities of writing to me as I am often wishing to hear from you all as I write to all directed to you, but I believe if any circumstances occurred, which often may, to prevent my sending to you, you would scarcely write once in seven years, and I have often observed you never write but on Sundays, surely you cannot be always be so much engaged in Business on other weekdays as not to be able to spare a quarter of an *[hour]* which I am sure is sufficient for what you generally write.

Our Regiment on its arrival from Spain was stationed at Horsham where I hoped it would remain, but before I was well enough to join they removed to Colchester and from thence to Ipswich where we shall in all probability remain until again ordered for foreign service. Had the Regiment remained at Horsham I should have obtained leave for a few days but as we are now about 70 miles from London the distance is too far to think of asking for it till next Winter should we be in England, as it is out of the power of Commanding Officers to grant furloughs at this time of year without urgent business may require it, and then leave must be obtained from the Commander in Chief of the forces, Horse Guards.

I hope you will give my kind respects to my uncle and Aunt, Sisters Jane and Mary and all our brothers friends and relations who I hope are well and happy.

I hope it will not be very long now if it please God I may live before I may expect my discharge as I shall soon have served

twenty one years and I am now getting much the worse for wear and the Spanish Expedition has considerably increased it,
    I remain Yr Affectionate Br
        Wm Kenward

    I hope Mr and Mrs Golber are well and your neighbours at Barkham.   WK

Letter 23
WK to JK at Moons   Ipswich 28th June 1809

Dear Brother
    We march from here of Monday next for Deal there to Embark for foreign Service, another secret Expedition, which I hope will be attended with better success than the former. I shall write no more possibly for some time but should like to hear how you all are before I leave England.
    My dutiful respects to uncle aunt Brothers Sisters relations & friends
        & remain yr Efft. Br.
            WK

Letter 24
WK Sergt 76th Hindoostan Foot to JK at Moons   Ipswich
                                                        19 February 1810

    I received your last about three weeks since and having nothing worth notice to mention omitted answering it till now, and am at present in the same state.
    We hear of nothing in this quarter but a report in circulation

of another expedition early next summer, and which I dare say will be the case and the Ipswich Brigade will most probably form a part thereof.

You mentioned a wish that I would procure a furlow, but I am sorry to say it is out of my power being very busy at present and the period of granting them will end in March next with a few exceptions.

We have a recruiting party marching this for Seaford, perhaps you way have seen them, they are under the Command of Lieut. Farncombe who comes from the neighbourhood of it.

Having nothing more to add but kind respects to uncle Aunt Brothers Sisters relations & friends.

I remain yrs. Effectionately
WK

I hope you have all enjoyed Christmas comfortably, this is I believe about the time you expected a visit from our Uckfield Cousins and I should be happy to pass an evening at cards with them also but it is utterly impossible. Don't forget my remembrance to them as also I Regard etc...

Letter 25
Sergt Kenward 76 Regt Foot to JK　　　Cork Barracks Ireland
　　　　　　　　　　　　　　　　　　　　8 August 1810

I again write informing you of my arrival here of the 27th Ulto. having left Ipswich 27th June our passage from Harwich were we embarked, was tedious altho short. The wind was many days against us, which obligded us twice to turn back to Dungeness having attempted to proceed on our short voyage to this land of potatoes.

I dare say I shall soon leave this for the isle of Wight and from thence to Madeira, having this day been inspected by

General Graham to whom I urged my request of being sent, who has not as yet given me his final answer. My new Commanding Officer wishes to persuade me from my determination but having once requested, and obtained the Commander in Chief's sanction, not all the world shall prevent me from obtaining that end. Whether it may better or worse me is a matter or indiference to me as also whether I die in Assia Africa America or Europe.

I have, you will allow, seen much, tho little indeed to make life a desireable Object and shall therefore part with it with less regret whenever it way be the will of the Almighty to call me from this world of trouble and Sorrow and I pray God we may so pass our lives on earth as to ensure a happy meeting in the mansions of bliss and eternity.

I will take it kind of you to answer this as soon as possible as perhaps I shall not be long here, direct as before to me at Cork, & give to my Uncle & Aunt and all our Brothers Sisters Relations & Friends my dutiful remembrance, and shall be happy to hear of all your health & happiness.

I remain your sincere & Effectionate Brother
                                                                WK

Letter 26
WK 2nd R.V.B and late Sergt.76th Regt to JK at Moons
(Scrap of letter)   Army Depot Isle of Wight
                                       28 February 1811

…………………..Fermoy in Ireland on 5th January last and embarked at Cork for this place on the 11th. We were six weeks on board owing to bad weather and contrary winds. How long I may remain here is uncertain but I fear much longer than wish, as there seldom or ever are any Vessels leaving this for Madeira. I cannot say that I am in any way partial to this place and shall be extremely happy of embracing the opportunity of leaving it.

It being so long since I last heard from Fletching that I hope that you will not fail to answer this with all convenient dispatch especially as my leaving this being so very uncertain, and, I hope sincerely of hearing that you all enjoy your health as thank God this leaves me, with the exception of now and then a slight fit of the Ague & feaver………..

………………………………..
…..………acquaintance etc etc.

You will I hope excuse the postage hereof. The Rule of this Garrison being to send all letters for the Commandants Signature open for his perusal, in consequence of which I have forwarded this from hence Unfranked

And remain Dear Brother, yours sincerely
WK

Letter 27
Sergt. 2nd RV Battn to JK at Moons

Cowes IoWight HM Ship Dido
Christmas Eve 24 Decr. 1811

Dear Brother

It being a considerable while since my last writing I now do it wishing you all a happy Christmas etc. and hope this will find you all in good health and a long continuance. I am nearly in the same state as at my last writing and had some thought of making application for a few weeks Furlow, but as I am at different uncertain times still perplexed with the Ague that I thought it advisable to drop the Idea until I see what next Summer may bring forth, when I should not join my Battn. or be discharged perhaps I may obtain it. At the same time must thank you for your offer, but am happy to say it would not be required should the Furlow have been obtained.

I have little to say as the place I am in does not circulate much news and I but seldom go on shore. The Capture of the Island of Java which you have long since heard of is a great acquisition to the India Company being the finest spice Island by far in the East as also for the produce of sugar Arrack etc. but very unhealthy.

I hope our uncle is better of his disorder than at your last writing and our aunt in good health, as also our Brothers Sisters & relations to all of whom give my kind respects also to Tom Redford & all acquaintances as formerly mentioned.

I shall expect to hear from you shortly and for the present conclude   Yr Effectionate Brother
WK

> This day twelve months I passed at Fermoy in Ireland
> This day two years on passage from the Island of Walcheren
> This day three years at Villa Franca in Spain
> This day four years in the Island of Jersey
> This day five years in the City of Lincoln
> This day six years at Point de Gaul in the Island of Ceylon East Indies
> - where I will be the next God only knows. Whether Dead or Alive or in what part concern me but little.

WK

Letter 28
WK Sergt 2RV Battn. to JK   Chatham Barracks
1 Nov 1814

Our battalion in part arrived in this garrison yesterday but for what purpose we as yet remain ignorant. We had a very dangerous passage from Madeira which we left 3rd Ultto. but fortunately the vessel in which I embarked arrived yesterday. Two others with parts of the Battalion are hourly expected. We may then know our fate or destination - some say we are to be retained, when I am more fully aqcuainted I shall write more fully - I expect in a few days to be ordered to Woolwich to deliver stores belonging to the late Garrison of Madeira having done the duty of Store Sergt. there. I shall for the present conclude in the hope this will find our Uncle Aunt and all friends well to whom give my kind respects.

    I am ……
    W. Kenward

This was of course before Napoleon escaped from Elba and the "Hundred Days", ending at Waterloo. The Army was being reduced and redeployed, much of it to North America.

William Kenward's Campaigns

The Second British-Mysore War 1789-1792

Following the death of Hyder Ali, the ruler of Mysore, in 1782 and the succession of his son Tipu Sultan, the First British-Mysore war was concluded in 1784.

However Mysore remained the major power in southern India, and Tipu, the Mahommedan ruler of a largely Hindu population, also ruled the Malabar coast north of Travancore and Cochin. The East India Company noted that "Tipu was the most active, powerful, ambitious prince of Hindustan, whose troops are in high order and whose powerful antipathy to the English is beyond what the Directors are yet well aware of." Furthermore in 1787 he had despatched an embassy to France and the French still aspired to expel the British from India. Although no French troops were actually sent to Mysore, Tipu had a number of French officers in his Army. Tipu was an obvious threat to the British and had to be dealt with before he reversed all that the British had achieved in southern India.

A rebellion in Malabar in 1789 had been suppressed by Tipu, but many people had fled south to Travancore and Cochin, enraging Tipu, who vowed to take his revenge on the Rajahs of Travancore and Cochin, to the alarm of the British administration. Tipu then invaded the terrritory of the Rajah of Travancore, a ruler friendly to the British. This was the start of the Second Mysore War.

Before the Mysore campaign proper started it was necessary for the Bombay army to secure its bases, which involved a preliminary campaign in Malabar to remove Tipu from the West coast. This was successful. In May 1790 Tipu, realising the strength of the forces combining against him, retreated to Mysore.

Sir Penderel Moon describes the situation: 'to understand the campaigns that followed, it must be remembered that the heart of Tipu's kingdom in which Mysore and his capital Seringapatam were situated was a large V-shaped plateau bounded on its two sides by mountain ranges, the Western and Eastern Ghauts, which converged as they ran southwards. Hyder Ali had added to his original kingdom the narrow coastal strip between the Western Ghauts and the sea, the southern portion of which was known as Malabar. The much broader plains below the eastern Ghauts were mostly part of the territory of the Nizam of the Carnatic, though Hyder Ali held some territory around Coimbatore.'

To come to grips with Tipu in his own domain, the British under Lord Cornwallis, the Governor-General, had to march armies, with all their heavy guns and equipment, up through the steep passes onto the Mysore plateau and then keep them supplied there. In face of a more numerous and more mobile enemy, operating on interior lines, this was no easy task, and partly explains why the British took so long to get the better of Tipu. His army probably numbered about 100,000, of which at least half were well trained men, well disciplined and much the best of all the Indian armies.'

The British had insufficient cavalry, and were supported by huge baggage trains, so they lacked Tipu's maneouvrability. The initial plan was for one British army under General Medows to strike from the south starting from Trichinopoly and occupying Coimbatore before climbing the Ghauts onto the Mysore plateau. Another army was to protect the Carnatic further north. Medows was however no match for Tipu and achieved little except the occupation of Coimbatore. Cornwallis now decided to take the field himself and tookover command with another army from Madras. In the meantime Abercromby and his small force from

Bombay, including the 75th, conquered Malabar.

At the beginning of 1791, Cornwallis and Medows advanced into Mysore from the east and captured Bangalore. However he could not press his advantage due to lack of supplies, and had to wait until May before advancing towards Seringapatam hoping to assault the fortress before the monsoon broke. Abercromby with the Bombay army and a battering train had meanwhile climbed the Western Ghauts, as described by WK, and was waiting the arrival of Cornwallis.

Progress towards Seringapatam was however slow, obstructed by Tipu's forces, and Cornwallis had barely reached the area when the rains started. He was unable to properly invest the fortress and, short of supplies due to Tipu's scorched earth policy, was forced to retreat. Abercromby, who had not yet joined up, was ordered to retreat back to Malabar. With unfortunate timing, just after the retreat started, a Mahratta army from the north joined Cornwallis with supplies, but as the monsoon was now well underway, he decided to continue his retreat.

This campaigning season thus ended without much British success, but Tipu was on the defensive, as it was still in the interests of both the Nizam of Hyderabad and the Marathas for Tipu to be defeated.

In January 1792, Cornwallis again advanced from Bangalore, reaching Seringapatam in February, while Abercromby climbed the Ghauts again to join him. However Cornwallis decided to attack immediately without waiting for the Bombay army, and Tipu, surprised and demoralised, gave up easily. Although Tipu had to meet quite severe peace terms, including giving up his two sons as hostages to the British, he lived to fight another day.

The Third British-Mysore War 1799

In 1798, Lord Wellesley became Governor General, and was firmly of the opinion that British interests were best served by an aggressive policy of extending British power and influence throughout India. Mysore under Tipu had recovered its confidence in the years since the last War, and Tipu was unwise enough to reopen communications with the French in Mauritius. These were in fact fairly minor in nature but were enough to enrage Wellesley, who resolved to attack Tipu as soon as possible. However an immediate campaign was impossible as the army needed months to prepare, so Wellesley took the opportunity to secure an alliance with Hyderabad. In the meantime, the French threat to India became much more credible with the arrival in Egypt of a French army under Napoleon.

By the beginning of 1799, Wellesley's preparations were complete, and the Madras army under General Harris set out from Vellore in February. As in the previous campaign, the Bombay army, under General Stuart, advanced over the Western Ghauts from Malabar, but was ordered not to descend from the mountains onto the Mysore plain until supported by cavalry from Harris's army.

Tipu's forces, although strong, were nothing like the numbers he had in the previous campaign, and he was slightly outnumbered by the British and Hyderabad forces combined. His strategy was to defeat the British forces in detail before they could combine, and deny them supplies. He attacked an isolated brigade of Stuart's army at Sedaseer Hill in the Western Ghauts, but was driven off by reinforcements, retreating to try his luck with General Harris, but without success. He then retired into the fortress of Seringapatam in the hope that his scorched earth tactics and the eventual arrival of the monsoon about the middle of May would protect him, as it had done before.

Tipu had strengthened the eastern defences but had done little to the western side so Harris saw his chance. He was well aware that he had little time for a protracted siege, and planned to assault the walls from the west rather than gaining a foothold on the island first as Cornwallis had done. Batteries were constructed to bombard the walls and Stuart's force, including the 75th, was placed north of the river to threaten the northwest corner.

After an abortive attempt to get Tipu to agree terms for a surrender, the bombardment was intensified and a breach made in the west wall. A storming party under General Baird overcame the defences after fierce fighting and the city fell, Tipu being killed. The city was given over to plunder by the victors, and General Arthur Wellesley, the Governor General's younger brother, had to work hard to restore order the next day. This was the end of Mysore as a significant power and threat to British advancement in India.

The Second British-Mahratta War 1803 - 1805

Following the death of Tipu, the main obstacle remaining to the British was the Mahratta Confederacy. The nominal head of the Mahrattas was the Peshwa, but the most powerful Rajahs were Sindia of Gwalior, Holkar of Indore, the Gaekwar of Baroda and the Rajah of Berar. Quarrelling among these Rajahs led to Holkar defeating the Peshwa at Poona, and he fled to British protection, signing a treaty with the British at Bassein. French influence with the Mahrattas was still a major concern to the British, and Governor General Wellesley decided on action. The Peshwa was reinstalled at Poona, and the British moved against the two main Mahratta forces, one in the Deccan under Scindia, and another further north under Holkar. The Southern command was given to General Arthur Wellesley, and the Northern command to General Lake.

The Southern campaign was quickly successful and effectively ended at the end of 1803, after a number of famous battles, including Assaye. The 75th took only a minor role in this campaign, operating mainly in Gujerat against the Gaekwar of Baroda, before being sent to join the Northern command under Lake.

Lake's campaign, in which the 76th played a prominent part, was initially successful, capturing Agra and Delhi, but Holkar did not give up and inflicted a major reverse on a force under Colonel Monson in August 1804. This put new life into the Mahrattas, and the British were forced to deploy larger forces. This strategy was successful and a number of fortressses were captured, until Lake came up against the very strong defences of Bhurtpore at the end of 1804. This siege was unsuccessful but by now the Mahrattas were losing confidence, and a peace was concluded in April 1805.

The Corunna Campaign 1808-1809

Napoleon's grand design to break Britain's command of the sea, unchallenged since Trafalgar, was to conquer the Mediterranean. An important part of this design was to conquer Iberia, Gibraltar and North Africa, and so in 1808 he invaded Spain and Portugal. However Spanish resistance encouraged the British government to come to the aid of Spain and a British army was landed in Portugal. Following Sir Arthur Wellesley's victory at Vimeiro and the disasterous Convention of Cintra which threw away all the subsequent advantage, Sir John Moore was appointed to command the army in Portugal.

In October 1808, he advanced into Spain, intending to join up with reinforcements under General Baird being landed at Corunna. Almost immediately, however, the huge problems caused by their Spanish allies became evident. Very little of what he had been promised in support ever materialised, as the Spanish provincial rivalries caused a breakdown of coordination between the various forces, with a total lack of realism on the part of the various Spanish generals. Moore pressed on to Salamanca where he became seriously worried that his small army was over exposed as, due to Spanish procrastination, Baird's progress towards a junction had been seriously delayed and Napoleon was advancing towards Madrid. He therefore decided to retreat but before he could do so, reports of Spanish determination to defend Madrid and pleas from the Spanish generals and the British Representative in Madrid, persuaded him to change his mind, and as soon as Baird joined him, to advance. Madrid however did fall to Napoleon without difficulty at the beginning of December, but Moore was still determined to help the Spanish, and calculated that if he could get east of the French, he could cut their communications and force Napoleon to retreat. His plan was to defeat Marshal Soult who was only a hundred miles away with a small army; the other French armies were thought to be many miles away in other parts of Spain.

Baird joined Moore at Astorga and the combined force pressed on to Sahagun. However it was now well into December and the first snows of the mountain winter were falling. Napoleon himself then took a hand and with his usual despatch, realised he could destroy Britain's only army if he could catch it unawares. He therefore collected all the forces he could and hurried north towards Moore.

Fortunately Moore was not where Napoleon thought him to be and, seeing his danger, decided on an immediate retreat. His army was turned round and hurried back to Astorga. By this time the French cavalry were in contact and Moore was faced with a race to get his army back behind the river Esla before being cut off. He made it by the skin of his teeth and the army, low on supplies, was then faced with a retreat across the snow covered Cantabrian Mountains to Corunna and safety, all the while being harried by the French who were determined not to let them escape. The following few weeks of struggle and privation, the successful battle to defend Corunna while the army was evacuated by the Royal Navy and the death of Moore are the stuff of legend.

The Walcheren Campaign 1809

The Expedition's main objects were to capture the strategic port of Antwerp and divert Napoleon's attention from Austria. The command was given to Lieutenant-General The Earl of Chatham, William Pitt's elder brother, with Admiral Sir Richard Strachan in command of the naval element. However the French were well aware of the value of the port and British preparations to launch an expedition. The defences were strengthened and reinforcements sent to the area and, even as the expedition sailed, word reached England of Austria's armistice with the French after the battle of Wagram. Napoleon was therefore free to send even more troops to defend Antwerp. If the British had acted with speed, success might have been attained, but the expedition was badly planned, delayed and muddled, and had missed its chance even before disease struck.

The original plan was to divide the force into three divisions, one to attack and capture the defences on the north bank of the Western Scheldt, the second to secure Cadsand opposite Flushing and the third to capture Flushing itself. Even as the expedition at last set off, confusion set in among the commanders and due to worsening weather, the planned occupation of Cadsand was called off, which allowed the reinforcement of the garrison of Flushing from the other side of the Scheldt.

The troops were eventually landed on Walcheren and Beveland, and after occupying the rest of Walcheren, Flushing was besieged. Although reinforced from across the river, it surrendered two weeks later. However, about the middle of

August, the British troubles began in earnest. The sea dykes in Walcheren had been broken, and although this did not save Flushing, the sodden ground and continual rain caused much hardship, and fever broke out. The naval and military commanders lost confidence in each other and quite soon Chatham, in view of the rapidly growing strength of the defences further upstream towards Antwerp and the fast increasing sickness of the troops, decided that Beveland should be evacuated and the army concentrated on Walcheren. By September it was plain that the expedition had failed. However Walcheren was not finally evacuated until December, by which time few men were fit for duty. The campaign had been a total disaster and a Parliamentary Inquiry was held. Perhaps the only thing that could be said is that it greatly worried Napoleon for a while and he made sure that, for the rest of the war, Antwerp was too strongly defended to be worth another attempt.

A piece of doggerel circulated in England afterwards shows the public view of the venture, as does a contemporary cartoon depicting the Earl of Chatham as "General Cheatem".

> "Lord Chatham with his sword undrawn
> Kept waiting for Sir Richard Strachan;
> Sir Richard, eager to be at 'em
> Kept waiting too - for whom? Lord Chatham."

Bibliography

Bryant Arthur *Years of Victory* Collins 1944.
Buddle Anne *The Tiger and the Thistle* National Gallery of Scotland 1999.
Cambridge History of India Vol 5. Ed. H.H.Dodwell Cambridge University Press 1929.
Cadell Sir Patrick *The Making of the Indian Princes* Oxford University Press 1943.
Dalrymple William *White Mughals* Harper Collins 2002.
Ellis M.H. *Lachlan Macquarrie - His Life, Adventures & Times* Angus & Robertson 1952.
Fortescue J.W. *A History of the British Army* Vols 3, 4 & 5. Macmillan 1902 - 1910.
Gardyne Lt.Col C.G. *The Life of a Regiment - The History of the Gordon Highlanders* Vols 1& 2. The Medici Society 1928.
Hayden Lt.Col F.A *Historical Record of the 76th "Hindoostan" Regiment* "The Johnson's Head" Lichfield 1908.
Recollections of Benjamin Harris (pub. as 'A Dorset Rifleman') Ed. E. Hathaway Shinglepicker 1995.
Hibbert Christopher *Corunna* Batsford 1961.
Hook Theodore *The Life of Gen. Sir David Baird* Bentley 1833
Holmes Richard *Redcoat* HarperCollins 2001.
Howard Martin R. *Walcheren 1809 : A Medical Catastrophe* British Medical Journal 1999.
Keay John *India - A History* HarperCollins 2000.
The Autobiography of Sgt. William Lawrence 1790-1869 (pub. as 'A Dorset Soldier') Ed. E. Hathaway Spellmount 1993.
Longford Elizabeth *Wellington - The Years of the Sword* Weidenfeld & Nicolson 1969.

Mackenzie Roderick (Lt. 52nd Regt.) *Sketch of the War with Tippoo Sultan* Private pubn. Calcutta 1794.
Manor Roll of Barkham 1828 Sussex County Record Office AMS2707.
Moon Sir Penderel *The British Conquest and Dominion of India* Duckworth 1989.
Nolan E.H. *The History of the British Empire in India* Vol. 2 Virtue 1878.
Shipp J. *The Path of Glory – Being the Memoirs of the Extraordinary Military Life of John Shipp.* Ed. C.J. Stranks. Chatto & Windus 1969.
The Letters of Private Wheeler Ed B.H.Liddell Hart. Michael Joseph 1951.
Wilkin W.H. *Life of Sir David Baird* George Allen 1912.

Index

Abercromby Col.Robert, 6, 14, 15, 16, 17, 139
Ackland Brig., 90
Agra, 67, 80
Aicotta, 13
Allahabad, 64, 65
Amedabad, 48
Amir Khan, 47
Antwerp, 92, 144, 145
Assaye, 76, 142
Astorga, 85, 143
Baird Sir David Gen., 27, 28, 29, 84, 86, 106, 141, 142
Bangalore, 16, 140
Barkham Manor, 2, 101
Barlow Sir George, 75
Barrington George, 9, 96
Bedanore, 35
Benares, 64, 65
Berhampore, 64
Betanzes, 84
Beverland, 93, 145
Bhurtpore Siege of, 69, 70, 71, 111
Bhurtpore Rajah of, 67, 68, 69, 70, 71, 111
Bombay, 3, 6, 7, 18, 26, 47, 62
Brahmins, 7
Braithwaite, Gen., 23
Brodera, 8, 54
Brown Col., 31
Buffallo, Prison Ship, 95
Burgo, 87
Burnet Col., 88

Calcutta, Ft. William, 62, 66, 75
Calicut, 25
Cambay, 47, 51
Cannanore, 14, 15, 16, 19, 21
Cannanore, Bibbee of, 15
Cannara Province, 35
Canoogee, 56
Cape of Good Hope, 5
Cawnpore, 63, 66, 75,
Chambers Lt., 14
Chatham Earl of, 90, 144, 145
Chatham, 3, 99, 135
Chelsea Hospital, 3, 100
Chitwa, 13
Chowghaut, 13
Clarke Col. Sir William., 46, 49, 50, 53
Cochin, 13, 25, 26, 137
Coimbatore, 14, 15, 21
Colchester, 83, 86, 125
Columbo, 26
Conojie, 56
Coorg, 16
Cork, 94, 133
Cornwallis Marquis and Governor-General, 14, 16, 17 20, 21, 31, 75, 138, 139
Corunna, 84, 86, 142, 143, 144
Cotiote, 40, 43, 46
Cotiparambo, 41
Cranganore, 13, 25
Craufurd Captain, later General, Robert, 5, 6, 21, 26,
Crowe N. Esq., Magistrate in Surat, 58
Cumine Lt.Col 75th Regt., 40
Cummer-ud-din Khan, 14
Danbury, 83
Dartford, 78, 113

Delhi, 67
Dido HMS, 95, 134
Dieg, 66, 67
Dinapore, 64
Dunlop Col 77th Regt., 29
East Grinstead, 3
East India Company, 4, 6, 19, 25, 34, 81, 137
Emslie Robert, Sergt., 74
Engel Capt. Paymaster 75th Regt., 73
England Gen., 88
Falmouth, 84
Fermoy, 94, 133
Fletching, 2, 134
Floyd, Brig. Gen., 14
Flushing, 90, 92, 144
Funchal, 96
Futtypore Siccra, 72
Gaekwar of Baroda, 47, 55, 56, 141, 142
Ganges River, 64, 65, 66
Gainsborough, 118
German Legion, 117
Ghazipore, 64, 75, 115
Goa, 46
Goddard Gen., 48
Gordon Maj. Gen., 96, 98
Graham Gen., 133
Graham Sergt., 29
Grant Lt., 31
Gray Maj. 75th Regt., 55
Great Mogul, 57, 67
Griffin Inn Fletching, 109, 119
Gujerat Province, 47
Harris Gen, 27, 140
Hartley Col., 13, 14
Harvey Lt. 75th Regt., 55

Harwich, 84, 90
Holford Mr., English Consul in Cambay, 52
Holkar, 47, 63, 67, 70, 80, 142
Holmes Lt.Col., 55
Hoogly River, 62
Hope Gen. Sir John, 86
Horse Guards, 74, 114, 130
Horsham, 94, 130
Hyder Ali, 21, 29, 31, 137, 138
Ipswich, 93, 94, 129, 131
Isard Mr., 2, 3, 103, 105, 106, 124
Isle of Wight, 94, 95
Jaffnapatam, 26
Jemaulabad, 35, 37
Jersey, 81, 119
Jones Gen, 68
Kennedy Sergt. Pat, 51
Kurria, 48, 51, 53, 108
Lady Castlereagh, East Indiaman, 76, 109
Lake Gen. Lord, 63, 66, 67, 70, 111, 141, 142
Laswarree, 67
Lawrence William, 4 4
Le Cannonier, French frigate, 76
Leith Maj.Gen., 85
Lewes, 101
Lincoln, 79, 81 79, 115
Lindsey Capt. 22nd.Regt., 71
Lord Duncan, East Indiaman, 76
Lugo, 84
MacRae Lt. Col. 76th Regt., 70, 117
Macquarie Lachlan, Capt 77th Regt., 23, 42
Madeira, 94, 95, 99, 133, 136
Madras, Ft St. George, 16
Madrid, 143
Mahe, 21

Maitland Lt. Col. 75th Regt., 68
Malabar, 13, 17, 25, 40
Mangalore, 35, 38, 43
Matthewson Lt.& Adj., 75th Regt., 73
McKenzie Maj.Gen., 85
M'Kenzie Capt. 75th Regt,. 20, 21
MColl Lt. 75th Regt., 55
Medows Gen., 16, 17, 139, 138
Middleburgh, 90, 92
Mignan Col., 27
Mole Lt., 55
Monghier, 64, 65
Monson Col. The Hon. 76th Regt., 69, 78, 80
Montana, 42, 43, 105
Montgomery Ensign, formerly Sergt. Major, 79, 80
Montresor Col., 35
Moons Farm Piltdown, 2, 103
Moore Gen. Sir John, 84, 85, 86, 142, 143, 144
Morgan Col., 117
Musgrove Gen. Sir Thomas, 94
Muttra, 67
Mysore, 13, 138
Napoleon, 44, 121, 130, 136, 140, 142, 144
Nerbudda River, 65
Newick, 2, 125
Nottingham, 78, 112, 114, 115
Numdedrooy, 35
Onore, 35
Parias, 10
Parker Mr., 49, 50, 54
Parsees, 9
Patna, 64, 66
Paulgautchery, 14
Periapatam, 16, 17
Piltdown, 101

Plymouth, 88, 128
Point De Galle, 76
Pollilur, Battle of, 29
Pondicherry, 23, 124
Ponsborne, East Indiaman, 4
Poodicherune Ghauts, 15
Portsmouth, 81
Prussian Army, 6
Pychee Rajah, 42
Pychee, 43
Regiments,
  8th Light Dragoons, 67, 71 72
  19th Light Dragoons, 20
  24th Dragoons, 72, 78
  27th Dragoons, 67
  2nd (Queens) Regiment, 90
  2nd Royal Veteran Battalion, 94
  12th Regiment ,31
  19th Regiment, 31
  22nd Regiment, 67, 71
  33rd Regiment, 31
  36th Regiment, 26
  51st Regiment, 85
  52nd Regiment, 26
  57th Regiment, 122
  58th Regiment, 122
  59th Regiment, 85
  60th Regiment, 84
  61st Regiment, 62
  65th Regiment, 70
  72nd Regiment, 26
  73rd Regiment, 16, 20
  74th Regiment, 4
  75th Highland Regiment, 3, 6, 16, 18, 20, 27, 28, 30, 32, 49, 53, 54, 57, 72, 74, 94, 110, 111, 124, 141, 142

76th Regiment, 62, 66, 67, 69, 72, 74, 84, 90, 108, 110, 122, 142
77th Regiment, 15, 16, 23, 25, 26, 29, 31, 42
84th Regiment, 46, 49, 50, 90
86th Regiment, 47, 54, 55, 70
87th Regiment, 72
88th Regiment, 47, 62
90th Regiment, 122
94th Regiment (Scotch Brigade), 31
Bengal European Regiment., 68, 72
Bombay European Regiment., 48, 68, 70
Bombay Marine Battalion, 47
Abercromby's Highlanders, 3
Duke of Wellington's Regiment, 4
Gordon Highlanders, 4
Highland Light Infantry, 4
Middlesex Regiment, 4
Sussex Militia, 120
West Middlesex Militia, 122
Rooth Lt.& Adj. 76th Regt., 86
Seaford, 132
Sedaseer Hill, 27, 140
Seringapatam, 14, 16, 17, 18, 20, 29, 32, 138, 139, 140
Sevendrooy, 35
Sheik Shabidar Tollerker, Subadar, 39
Shipp Sergt John., later Ensign, 72, 76, 78
St Helena, 76, 77, 110
St Iago di Compostella, 84, 85
St. Iago, Canary Islands, 4
Stirling, 2, 3
Strachan Admiral Sir Richard, 144, 145
Stuart, Gen., 26, 27, 142
Surat, 52, 57
Surrey, East Indiaman, 76
Sutherland Drum Major 75th Regt., 53

Suttee, 9
Symes Lt.Col 76th Regt., 80, 87
Temple Capt. 86th Regt., 55
Thornton Gen., 116
Tillichery, 40, 41, 43, 46
Tipu, 13, 14, 21, 25, 28, 35, 105, 137, 138, 139, 140, 141
Travancore, 13, 137
Trevanagary, 14
Trincomallie, 26
Upper Provinces, 63
Uckfield, 132
Veere, 90
Veitch Mr. Consul in Madeira, 99
Vellore, 30
Vigo, 85
Vizier Ali, 65
Walcheren, 90, 93, 144, 145
Walker Maj., 47
Walpole East Indiaman, 76
Watson Lt.Col. 75th Regt.,, 59
Wellesley Col. Arthur, 27, 30, 67, 80
Wellesley Marquis, Governor-General, 75, 140
Wellington Duke of, 92, 93, 98
Weston Lt., 55
Williamson Capt., 48, 53
Wood Mr. Fletching Schoolmaster, 2
Woodington Col.,54
Woolwich, 136
York Duke of, 114